A POCKET HISTORY OF
SCOTLAND

A POCKET HISTORY OF
SCOTLAND

Gill Books

Contents

Out of the Ice

Scotland has a long and fascinating geological history that has been at least three billion years in the making.

Over the years, Scotland's land has travelled along the earth's tectonic plates and experienced desert, tropical and volcanic climates, as well as several ice ages.

Around 600 million years ago, the British Isles began life split in two, with Scotland and northern Ireland joined together as part of a massive continent with North America. On the other side of an ocean, southern Ireland, England and Wales formed part of a separate continent – the two continents were slowly moving towards each other. At this point Scotland, and the rest of Britain, lay far south of the equator.

STAFFA
These rock formations were created from cooling volcanic lava.

The continents gradually came together over millions of years; at first to form the mass continent of Pangaea, and then – as it split apart and sea levels rose – they eventually became the islands we recognise today.

LOCH NESS
Scotland's most famous loch was formed by the movement of the Great Glen Fault over millions of years.

Scotland's landscape has been shaped by ferocious ice ages. Vast sheets of ice would have covered the country, with glaciers scraping through the land, gouging out valleys and raking away rock. Evidence of this can be seen today with the abundance of boulder clay (eroded rock material) that covers much of the country, and the large boulders, appearing as if from nowhere, that would have been transported by an ice age glacier.

Before the Mid-Atlantic Ridge formed and the continents of Europe and North America became separate, Scotland was sandwiched between the two continents and its land was split in two by a huge fault line – the Great Glen Fault.

The movement of the fault line displaced the land and is responsible for much of Scotland's landscape. As the tectonic plates on either side of the fault shifted, mountain ranges were formed and valleys were cut into the landscape. Erosion caused by the movement of the fault line formed Scotland's most famous loch, Loch Ness. The Great Glen Fault is considered inactive, although mild tremors were observed in 1934.

The first known settlers in Scotland would have arrived after the final ice age, when early humans began to look for fresh sources of food and while a land bridge still connected the British Isles to the rest of Europe. Evidence suggests that

FIRST SETTLERS
In Scotland would have arrived after the final ice age and learned to hunt using a stone blade most likely attached to a wooden spear.

the earliest settlers would have lived in caves, often by the shores, and survived on a diet of nuts, berries, seeds, root vegetables and seafood. As people began to understand their resources, populations grew and settlements emerged. These early communities lived in harmony with the land, hunting meat with a typical Mesolithic stone blade that was most likely attached to a wooden spear. There is evidence to suggest that communities met and socialised together, which would have aided breeding with non-relatives and the widening of the gene pool.

There may have been earlier settlers, but any evidence and genealogy would have been wiped out by volcanic activity and ice ages. These early settlers developed techniques and ways of living off the land that would lead to the first farmers of the Neolithic age.

SUILVEN
One of the oldest and most famous geological landmarks in Scotland.

The First Farmers

Farming was first discovered in the Middle East around 6,000 BC. It took thousands of years for the concept to travel north and finally reach Scotland.

The reason for the eventual move to farming in Scotland is unknown. It could have been invaders from southern Europe who brought their knowledge with them, or simply farmers from the south searching for new land to cultivate, or it could have been a realisation that there was an easier way to cultivate food than just

living from what became available through nature; the need for a reliable source of food would have increased with a growing population.

Previous generations had been nomadic, living from the earth and moving camp when resources became low. The invention of farming, however, led to the emergence of permanent villages and settlements, with people staying in one place. These people became known as Neolithic people, meaning 'New Stone Age'. They eventually devised a system of ownership; some stone structures from this period can still be found today, although it is thought that most of the settlements would have been built from timber.

From these early settlements, villages emerged. The best evidence of this is in the preserved Neolithic village of Skara Brae. The buildings at Skara Brae give a great insight into what life might have been like for Neolithic farmers. Buildings here were made out of stone and were not built very tall (people would have been shorter than today).

NEOLITHIC TOOLS
Were fashioned from stone, chipped into a rough shape, then polished with an abrasive rock.

Passageways joined many of the buildings, although they were designed in such a way that each family would have been able to close a door to gain privacy.

It is from this period that the earliest evidence of arts and crafts emerged. The discovery of farming meant that for the first time in history, a species did not use 100 per cent of its efforts simply to survive. With leisure time available to many of the villagers, some buildings may have been used for honing craft skills such as carpentry and pottery. This led inevitably to the pursuit of pleasure through arts, crafts and sports. During this time, new religious practices came into vogue and new rituals and systems of belief emerged. Ceremonial sites, such as stone circles, were often constructed close to the villages, some believe for the celebration of the rituals. However, the true reason for the building of these stone circles may never be known.

SKARA BRAE
Has been described as the most perfect stone age village in Europe. It was remarkably well preserved in the sand that covered it for so many centuries.

Some think they were built as monuments to the dead, while others believe they had a more spiritual purpose. It is interesting to note that many stone circles (such as Stonehenge in England) often line up with the sun during the summer solstice.

STONE CIRCLES
May have been built for religious ceremonies, to honour the dead, or as a way of keeping time.

Neolithic people also built large, communal tombs made from huge slabs of rock. Some tombs had a passage leading to an inner chamber, while others were covered by stones and earth to create a mound. Recent evidence and carbon dating has suggested that the earliest remains found were actually interred hundreds of years after the construction of the tombs. Perhaps we will never know the original intended use of these structures.

The Celtic Age of Iron

The term Celtic is often used to describe the early medieval, and often Christian, people of the British Isles.

Metalwork was introduced to Scotland after around 2,500 BC. It is thought travelling craftsmen and a new wave of settlers brought this knowledge with them. The metal ores, first copper, then bronze and, finally, iron, had to be heated to extremely high temperatures so that they could be moulded. Weapons and tools were the most common products made.

CELTIC WARRIOR
From the later period, when swords and armour were more common.

During this time, the population grew and those in power used this new-found material to display their wealth. Small rectangular buildings were replaced with brochs – round, hollow-walled structures often surrounded by smaller dwellings. It was first thought by archaeologists that these were used as defensive forts, but a more popular theory

BROCHS
Were originally assumed to be defensive forts.

is that they were the houses of a landowner who held authority over the rest of the community. Brochs are also referred to as 'duns' in the west.

The early Celts soon discovered bog iron, the ore needed to make iron. Although the nature of a weapon suggests they were made for fighting, there is no evidence of warfare until around AD 700 when written records appear.

Around the same time, the invention of the wheel had made its way north and Scots began making carts and grain grinders.

Before the arrival of Christianity, the early Scots attempted to understand the mysteries of the world for themselves, often worshipping nature itself.

Archaeological finds from this time suggest that people made offerings to the earth that were either buried or thrown into the water. Unlike the druids in Britain and Ireland, it is unlikely that the Celts took part in human sacrifice, although it is thought they may have extracted body parts from the deceased for 'good luck'.

BRONZE AGE
Artifacts have been discovered by archaeologists throughout Scotland.

The people of the iron age wore colourful clothing and made intricate metal ornaments, incorporating the knotwork that is today associated with the Celts. It is widely accepted that the various Celtic tribes that existed in Scotland enjoyed storytelling, feasting and drinking an early form of beer, or mead. Social status was often directly related to the amount of ale a person could consume. The more important he was, the larger his drinking vessel would be.

As the population grew, many tribes were pushed out into more undesirable areas, such as hills and rugged coastlines, which may have caused tension to grow between tribes. The different tribes became more numerous and distinct from one another. Although this may have caused minor conflict, complex forms of social hierarchy were becoming apparent. Today, many examples of crannogs (ancient loch-dwellings built on stilts driven into the loch bed) and hill forts, built to accommodate the shifting population and defend it where necessary, still exist.

CRANNOG
An often circular home built on stilts and situated on a loch.

Calgacus and Mons Graupius

The Romans arrived in Scotland around AD 83, 40 years after the Roman invasion of England, which took place in AD 43.

CALGACUS' SPEECH

A sketch depicting the speech of Calgacus to the Caledonians at the Battle of Mons Graupius.

They had decided to venture further north and conquer the rest of the British Isles. Their push north can be traced by following the building of Roman forts and roads along the way.

Agricola, the Roman governor at the time, began to send military fleets into Scotland – or as they called it at the time – Caledonia. A chieftain named Calgacus led the Caledonian army in the Battle of Mons Graupius. The Roman soldiers would have been used to conquering land and dealing with barbarian soldiers, and although the Caledonians had the advantage of higher ground and more men, the Roman army quickly cut down the men and easily outflanked

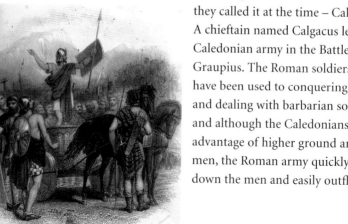

THE LEGEND OF CALGACUS

Calgacus was allegedly the leader of the Caledonian army that fought the Romans in the Battle of Mons Graupius. He is famously the first person to be referred to as a 'Scot'. In writings by the Roman historian at the time, Tacitus, he is credited with giving a speech about the Roman Empire that included the famous line: 'Plunder, slaughter and robbery they falsely call empire; they make a desert and call it peace.'

However, it is likely that Calgacus' speech may have been made up, or exaggerated for a more exciting story, as he would have spoken in Old Welsh rather than measured Roman phrases.

SCOTLAND
Came under attack for the first time from the Romans, who had already conquered England.

them. The Caledonians retreated into the woods; many were pursued and killed by Roman soldiers, although a great many also escaped.

The location of the Battle of Mons Graupius (Latin for the Grampian Mountains) is a subject of constant speculation, with many differing opinions. No archaeological evidence has emerged to favour any one

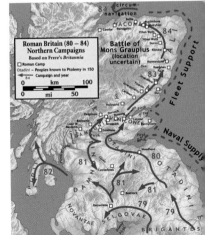

Roman Britain (80 – 84)
Northern Campaigns
Based on Frere's *Britannia*

☐ Roman Camp
Otadini – Peoples known to Ptolemy in 150
➤ 84 – Campaign and year

0   km   100
0   mi   50

Battle of
Mons Graupius
(location
uncertain)

BATTLE OF MONS GRAUPIUS
Where the Scots were easily defeated by highly trained Roman soldiers.

site in particular. For this reason, the site of the battle remains hotly contested and is still under investigation; Historic Scotland has yet to suggest a definitive location.

Following the battle, the Romans claimed to have conquered all the tribes of Britain; however this was not strictly true, as they had not reached the northern territories. The Romans continued to build forts, believed to have been intended either to

facilitate further attacks in Scotland, or to control existing conquered territory. However, a few years later, after Agricola left his position of governor in AD 85, his soldiers abandoned forts north of the Tay and returned to the area in which Hadrian's Wall was later built.

The intended conquest of Caledonia had failed in its mission to incorporate the northern tribes into the Roman Empire.

Romans vs Britons and Picts

Although the Romans had failed to conquer Scotland, they soon realised that they needed to protect the empire that they still controlled.

In AD 122 the building of Hadrian's wall, named after the emperor at the time, began. The wall measured 73 miles (120 km) and stretched from Wallsend, near the River Tyne in the east, to the village of Bowness-on-Sulway in the west.

HADRIAN'S WALL
Was the most fortified defensive line ever built by the Romans.

The wall was considered the most fortified defensive line in Europe and, while at the time it would have been a border between the Roman province of Britannia and the barbarian tribes of the north, today the wall lies in England, 20 miles (32 km) south of the Scottish border at its nearest point. Although many believe the wall was built purely as a military defence to keep the northern tribes out and to protect the empire from rebellion in Roman Britain, it was also likely to have served as a customs point, where tax could be collected on any trade between communities on either side of the border.

After Hadrian's death, the Emperor Antonius advanced north, beyond Hadrian's Wall. It is thought his aim was to bring northern tribes into the Roman Empire and to keep a watchful eye beyond the new frontier at the Forth-Clyde isthmus. The Romans set about building roads, forts and another defensive barrier – the Antonine Wall.

ANTONIUS
The emperor credited with extending the Roman Empire to its northernmost point.

TRIMONTIUM
This would have
been the site of a
Roman fort during
the years AD 80–240.

This wall was built across what is now known as
the Central Belt of Scotland and represented the
northernmost point of the Roman Empire, if only
for a short while.

WHO WERE PICTS?

Picti was a Roman nickname given to the peoples who
lived beyond the rivers Forth or Tay. The exact boundary is
not clear. The name appears to cover different peoples at
different times; for example, the Caledonians also appear
to have been regarded as Picts, rather than one people.
The people beyond the Forth or Tay were subject to
less Roman surveillance and influence. From the Roman
perspective, that made them more barbarous and wild.
Both the threat from the Romans and the subsequent
control of the lucrative trade routes to the empire may have
led to the formation of larger tribal confederations, which
laid the foundations for the later kingdoms of the Picts.
The Picts had their own language, which was a form of
Old Welsh – Brythonic. Picts also used a series of symbols
carved into stone; the meaning of these symbols remains
unknown, but can still be seen on Pictish symbol stones
throughout northern Scotland.

The Antonine Wall is less well known than Hadrian's Wall, perhaps because it was built from turf and stone and so has not been as well preserved, and also because the Roman conquest of this part of Scotland did not last long; the Romans eventually abandoned the wall and returned to their former frontier. By AD 160, Hadrian's Wall once again served as the boundary. Despite their failure to conquer, what did survive was the notion of a new religion – Christianity. By the end of the third century, the Roman Empire began to crumble and it didn't take long for Britain to declare its independence from Rome. During their struggle for control, the Romans had inadvertently amalgamated the northern tribes into larger units, laying the foundations for the later Christian kingdoms that would dominate the history of Scotland for the next five centuries. In the north lay the Picts, in the south the Britons, in the West were the newly arrived Gaels and in the South East, the Angles.

CONSTANTINE
The Roman emperor who introduced Christianity into the Roman Empire.

Columba and Iona

The story of early Christianity in Scotland is thought to have first developed with Roman ideas of Christianity.

COLM CILLE
Also known as Columba – Scotland's 'Father of Christianity'.

Although the Romans never truly conquered Scotland, they would have held cultural sway over its people; southern parts of the country that were conquered at some point would certainly have adopted some Roman ways of life. The Emperor Theodosius the Great made Christianity a state religion in the 380s. The first evidence of Christianity north of Hadrian's Wall appeared in the fifth century in the form of carved stones inscribed with crosses. After the fall of the Roman Empire, Britain was left to develop its own distinctive brand of Celtic Christianity, which soon spread to Ireland. Little is known about the religious practices of the Picts at this time, although they would presumably have practised pagan religions or a form of polytheism. The Christianisation of Scotland happened over many centuries, with old pagan traditions merging with new Christian beliefs.

Missionaries began to arrive in Scotland around the fourth and fifth centuries. The first missionary was Ninian, a man from Britain with Roman connections. He is believed to have established a Christian church in Scotland in the area of Whithorn, Dumfries and Galloway. The name Ninian was derived from the original name Uinniau, because the letters 'u' and 'n' looked almost identical in writings of that time.

Although Ninian was the first missionary, it is Columba who is recognised as the father of Christianity in Scotland. Columba was an Irish

IONA ABBEY
The Abbey of Iona, in the Western Isles of Scotland.

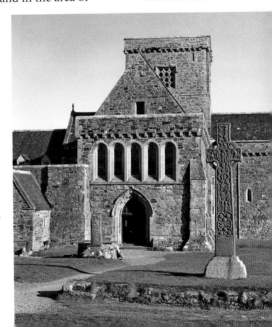

ST PATRICK
Many historians believe he originated from northern Britain, possibly even Scotland. He returned to this area later in life, which may have influenced the Christianisation of Scotland.

monk who had argued with other Irish monks; these arguments escalated into a battle in which many men were killed. Because of this Columba exiled himself and travelled to Scotland, where he was granted the island of Iona by a Gaelic king, and set up his own monastery.

His influence in Scotland, through Christian teaching, mediation between feuding tribes and allegedly performing miracles, spread Christianity through a still very pagan Scotland.

The island of Iona became the main centre of learning in Scotland and, as word spread, Columba became famous, not just as a missionary, but as a diplomat and scholar. He would have been held in great esteem, as most people in Scotland at that time, including many kings, had not yet learnt to read or write. Columba brought with him the skill of literacy. Churchmen became powerful because

they were often the only people who could write at this point. Monks would have created all the written accounts from this period and it was they who now had the power to shape Scotland's history and the image we have of Columba. Columba's insular brand of Christianity was falling out of favour as the Church began to standardise customs. It was Adomnán, an abbot of Iona, and his book, 'Life of Columba', written nearly one hundred years after Columba died, that made him into the Christ-like figure we know today and, as a result, Iona grew in importance.

Despite hardly leaving his abbey in Iona, Columba is credited with reviving Christianity in Scotland. Columba died on Iona and was buried in the abbey by his monks.

ST AUGUSTINE
His writings influenced the development of Christianity in western Europe; he is responsible for the concepts of original sin and just war.

ST NINIAN
Regarded as Scotland's earliest saint.

The Pictish Kingdom

KEILLOR SYMBOL STONE
Thought to represent the dynasty of a line of Pictish kings.

The Picts were people who inhabited the northern part of ancient Scotland, which was also known by the Romans as Caledonia.

Little is known about the origin or way of life of the Picts before the Roman invasions, as there was no way of recording history until that point. Picti is the name given to the confederation group of tribes first by the Romans and later by the Irish Annalists, but it is not actually known what they called themselves. Many historians believe that the Pictish people were made up of many different tribes who were effectively forced to come together because of the threat of Roman invasion, which they fiercely opposed.

Pictland was not ruled over by one king; in fact, there were two main kingdoms or power blocks that may have been subdivided.

THE PICTS AND THE FLAG OF SCOTLAND

St Andrew, the patron saint of Scotland, and the flag of Scotland are alleged to have Pictish origins. It comes from a story about the Pictish King, Óengus II, who is often referred to as playing a key role in the founding of the religious areas of Dunkeld and St Andrews. This stems from a victory that St Andrew helped the Picts to secure and in appreciation they regarded him as a saint. It is believed that the Picts kept possession of his holy bones and that the flag design, featuring the Saltire of St Andrew, emerged from this event.

No matter how many kingdoms there were, it is clear that the Picts controlled much of eastern and northern Scotland. The land in this region was fertile and productive. Pictish leaders would have accumulated great wealth from taxation of crops, which enabled them to commission distinctive art that was carved into stone.

Although the Picts were considered an insular population, there is evidence of trade with the Britons and with the Gauls in northern Europe, as well as with the Gaels living in the west of Scotland in the

ABERLEMNO CROSS
Shows the intricate art of the Picts.

PICTISH KNIFE
Featuring the 'Z-rod' design, a symbol often carved on Pictish artefacts.

kingdom known at that time as Dál Riata. The Picts are likely to have practised their own pagan religion, but they slowly converted to Christianity, taking on customs as they became convenient.

Pictish kings were powerful, but the ambiguous nature of the order of succession meant that the throne was often contested; this often led to fierce competition for power, frequently ending with political executions.

In the west, the small Gaelic kingdom of Dál Riata soon began to feel the full force of Pictish power. In 741 the Picts

stormed their fortress at Dunadd and reduced their kings to vassal status, a situation which would last for the next century. In 685, the Picts had also finally defeated the powerful Northumbrians at the battle of Dunnichen, ensuring that the Pictish high kings dominated northern Britain.

PICTISH COMMUNTIES
Co-existed peacefully alongside each other and often traded and intermarried.

But in 834, a Norse army wiped out the main Pictish royal line in one battle. And it was a Gaelic vassal, Cináed mac Alpin (Kenneth Mac Alpin), who established his rule in 843. He founded a Gaelic dynasty that would rule as kings of the Picts for decades. He also moved power from Iona, which was exposed to Viking raids, to Dunkeld, the site of an ancient Caledonian fort in Perthshire.

In 878, Kenneth's dynasty was overthrown and replaced by a usurper, Giric. This accelerated the cultural takeover of Pictland and soon Gaelic traditions, language and religion became commonplace. By the end of the ninth century, Pictland no longer existed.

The Vikings

During the late eighth century, Viking longships made their approach around the northern coast of Scotland – heading towards the Western Isles.

VIKING WARRIORS
First raided Scotland
in AD 794.

The Vikings came from the countries of Scandinavia. Lack of agricultural land and a growing population sent them on a quest for new land in the west. The Vikings were skilful raiders, traders and settlers. They travelled far and wide in their search for new land to settle, with some reaching parts of North America. Viking raids were brutal and would have taken place on a large scale. The first Viking raid happened at the English monastery at Lindisfarne in Northumbria in 793. This was followed a year later by the first Scottish raid on the holy island of Iona. It didn't take long for the Vikings to learn to navigate their way through the rivers of Scotland and into the heart of the Scottish kingdom, putting the final nail in the coffin of the already faltering Pictish kingdom.

ORKNEY ISLANDS
Became the first Norse settlements in Scotland.

Despite conquering parts of mainland Scotland, the Vikings chose to settle in the Northern Isles of Shetland and Orkney, as well as the Hebrides and the Isle of Man. After the initial plundering, Viking settlers tended to integrate into the Gaelic way of life, with many even adopting Christianity. The Vikings brought with them their own social order. The leader of each area was called a jarl – 'jarl' being the Norse origin of the word 'earl'.

The Jarl of Orkney was granted power by the king of Norway. The first known jarl, or earl, of Orkney was Rognvald Eysteinsson; all future earls were directly descended from Rognvald.

Back home in Norway, the Vikings had problems of their own, and many disagreed with the rule of King Harald Fairhair. Most of the Viking settlers had fled because of Harald's rule and were now plotting against him and planning to attack their native country. Harald fought back at the settlers and easily quashed the rebellion. This meant that the Hebrides, Northern Isles, Isle of Man and parts of Scotland now fell under Norwegian rule.

The Vikings of the Isles, however, set up their own kingdom, often rebelling against Norwegian rule – the first to declare himself 'King of the Isles' was Ketil Flatnose.

KING HARALD FAIRHAIR

His rule forced many Vikings to leave their homeland and raid the British Isles.

The kings of the Isles ruled almost independently, entered defensive deals and alliances with the kings of Scotland and frequently resisted control by Norway.

Over time the Vikings in the Hebrides became part of Gaelic society, however Orkney and Shetland remained under the control of the Norwegian kings until 1468.

Viking heritage is still remembered and celebrated in Scotland, particularly in the Northern Isles.

VIKING HELMET
According to Norse tradition, all men were required to own weapons and armour.

UP HELLY AA
Festival takes place every January in Lerwick, Shetland, and celebrates the Viking traditions once practised on the island, including galley burning.

The Kingdom of Alba

The Pictish kingdom merged with the Gaelic kingdom of Dál Riata, forming the kingdom of Alba, which included Britons and Anglo-Saxons living there.

KENNETH MAC ALPIN
King of Gaels and Picts.

DONALD II
The first King of Alba.

The Kingdom of Alba was the name for Scotland from around 889; gradually the English language name, Scotland, came to dominate. Initially the Dál Riatan rulers had overpowered the Pictish kingdom, but after they failed to defend the country from Viking invasions their dynasty was undermined.

Kenneth Mac Alpin (or Cináed mac Alpin) became King of the Scots and the Picts around 843. As the Vikings began to take over areas of Scotland and the Western Isles, the Scots – formerly of Dál Riata – lost the support of their Gaelic allies in Ireland. With the combined threat of the Vikings gaining more territory and the Anglo-Saxon threat from the south, the Pictish and Dál Riatan kingdoms were forced to consolidate, and the kingdom of Alba was formed.

Viking invasions on the east coast of England

weakened Anglo-Saxon control over Northumbria and Lothian and Alba gradually expanded, regaining these territories for the country.

The lack of historical records from that time make it impossible to know exactly how Alba came to be. However, the most common understanding is that the main tribes living in the land came together and merged their cultures over time; the catalyst for this being the threat of invasion, first by the Romans, then the Saxons and, finally, the Vikings.

For the residents of the new kingdom, life would have stayed the same, and they may not even have been aware of the merging of the two kingdoms. The political divide was still apparent and took on physical form in the Grampian Mountains, which still divided the two former kingdoms. Vikings who had settled in the west took on the Gaelic ways of life and customs,

STONE OF SCONE
The coronation stone used by all Scottish monarchs since the beginning of the Dál Riatan dynasty.

even adopting
Christianity.

Christianity
and the Church
played a key
role in bringing
the kingdoms
together – shared
beliefs helped to
lessen rivalries and
promote economic
growth. However,

DUNNOTTAR CASTLE
The scene of
many battles
for the kingdom.

Christianity had flourished in the old kingdom of
Dál Riata, and although Iona remained an important
location, the takeover of the Pictish kingdom meant
that power shifted to the east and a new religious
centre in Dunkeld emerged.

Because the people lived in separate centres
of population, the administration of the country
remained localised, with the ordinary people living off
the land and the elite rulers imposing taxes that had to

be paid either in food or in hospitality – coinage had not yet found its way into Scottish culture at this time.

Kenneth Mac Alpin was succeeded by his son, Aed, who was succeeded by his brother, Constantine. Donald II may then have been the first king to actually hold the title of King of Alba in 1093. For many, this alteration in the naming tradition signals the official birth of Scotland. However, it was Donald II's successor, Constantine II, who would become famous as a pivotal figure in the formation of the kingdom of Alba, the core of which would become Scotland.

MALCOLM I
King from 943-54.

CAMUS' STONE
Marks the important victory of King Malcolm II over the Vikings and the death of their leader, Camus.

Constantine mac Aed

Constantine II is thought of by many as the first King of Alba, although his elder cousin Donald preceded him to this title.

During Constantine's reign, the country was still under constant threat from raiding Vikings. At first, it looked as if his rule was under threat, but he recovered from a surprise attack to defeat the Vikings in 904. He sought to extend his power into northern England and a new struggle emerged over which king would control the crumbling Viking territory of Northumbria; his main rival was Athelstan, the Anglo-Saxon king of Wessex. Athelstan conquered Northumbria and Constantine was forced to form an alliance with Athelstan in recognition of his power. Soon the two kings were often at war. Constantine forged an

CONSTANTINE II
King of Alba after the death of his cousin, Donald.

alliance with Britons, Northumbrians and Vikings and it is this conflict that culminated in the battle of Brunanburh.

As in the case of Mons Graupius, the battle site of Brunanburh is unknown – although many historians believe it to have been at Bromborough on the Wirral Peninsula in England. The battle was one of England's most important victories as it united various parts of the country – it is likely to have been extremely bloody with a massive loss of life. According to historic records, Constantine lost a son in battle. The victory was costly for Athelstan and his defences were severely weakened. The battle shaped the territories that are still occupied today by the various countries that make up the British Isles, as each kingdom

CHURCH AT MOOT HILL
Commemorates the place where Constantine pledged himself to the law of the church.

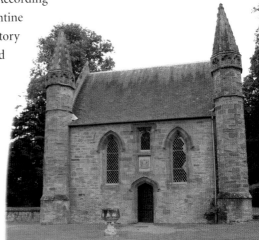

BATTLE OF BRUNANBURH
The first of many battles between the English and the Scots.

involved retreated to consolidate the dominions they possessed.

Athelstan died only a year later and his successor, his brother Edmund, spent most of his reign rebuilding the war-torn empire.

Despite a successful reign, Constantine abdicated the throne, perhaps under pressure

from his nephew, Malcolm, who was next in line to the throne. (Although Constantine had a son, kingship alternated between two branches of the family so that there was always an adult successor, because their job would often be to lead the country into battle. The son did not usually inherit the kingdom, but would then be next in line.)

Hail Macbeth

Macbeth is best known as the subject of Shakespeare's famous play; however, that story does not provide an accurate portrayal of his reign.

Macbeth was the son of Findlaech, who was Mormaer (king) of Moray. It is thought that Macbeth's mother was the daughter of Malcolm II.

Malcolm II was instrumental in securing victory over the Angles in the south and for bringing Lothians under Scottish rule. Following Malcolm's death, Macbeth and his wife, Gruoch, had reason to believe that their royal lineage, together with Macbeth's experience of ruling the independent Moray, would mean that they would succeed Malcolm to the throne.

However, Duncan, the son of another of Malcolm's daughters, laid his claim to the throne. It is likely that Duncan claimed the throne over

SHAKESPEARE
Used the legend of Macbeth as material for one of his best-known tragedies.

Macbeth because he had already claimed the throne of Strathclyde; when the King of the Britons of Strathclyde died without a successor, Duncan was quick to establish a kingdom.

Duncan's claim to the Scottish throne after Malcolm II's death meant that the Scottish kingdom extended even further south than it does today.

Duncan's reign was not easy and early military blunders fuelled Macbeth to challenge the throne. As the independent ruler of Moray, Macbeth posed a certain threat to Duncan, and in 1040, Duncan marched his army north to challenge Macbeth.

Duncan was killed in battle and Macbeth became king. Macbeth's claim to the throne was unchallenged and Duncan's wife fled Scotland with her children. Macbeth moved the throne north-east to his stronghold of Moray, which may have had a positive effect in uniting the two sides of Scotland that lay on either side of the Grampian Mountains.

KING MALCOLM'S GRAVESTONE, AT GLAMIS.

MALCOLM II
King Macolm II's gravestone at Glamis.

Although Macbeth's reign was, for the most part, unchallenged, he did face hostility from the Norse-influenced Earls of Orkney and also from the Earl of Northumbria. But his eventual downfall came at the hands of Malcolm III, Duncan's son.

Northumbria lay just south of the Scottish kingdom and would have felt threatened by the increasing power of the Scottish kingdom and by Macbeth's shifting of the throne to Moray. The Earl of Northumbria, personified by Macduff in Shakespeare's tragedy, instigated an invasion of Scotland in 1054. The earl had joined forces with Malcolm, who most probably lived most of his life in England, having left Scotland after his father's death. Malcolm seized this opportunity to avenge his father's death, killing Macbeth.

Macbeth's son, Lulach (known as 'Lulach the Fool'), inherited the throne. However, his very short reign came to an end when he was killed by

DUNCAN I
Beat Macbeth to the throne after the death of Malcolm II.

Malcolm, who was crowned King Malcolm III in 1058. Malcolm married an English princess, Margaret, after granting asylum to her and her brother Edgar, the Anglo-Saxon heir to the English throne, following the Norman Conquest of England in 1066. Thanks to a long line of male descendants and a strengthening of the political infrastructure, Malcolm's reign marked the end of years of royal rivalry. However, his involvement of the English territory of Northumbria in his quest for the throne marked the moment when English influence was invited into Scotland for the first time.

On the pretext of supporting his brother-in-law's claim to the English throne, Malcolm invaded England five times and was killed in battle at Alnwick, Northumberland, in 1093.

MALCOLM III
Avenged his father's death by killing Macbeth in 1054.

Two Kings Who Made Scotland

David I and Alexander II are the two kings considered responsible for the eventual Normanisation of Scotland.

EDINBURGH CASTLE
Developed by David I as a site of royal power.

JEDBURGH ABBEY
Founded by David I in 1138.

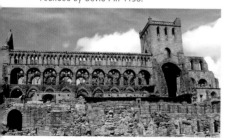

David I was the youngest son of Malcolm III; he challenged his nephew for the throne following the death of his brother, Alexander I. It is believed that time spent in England and the backing of the English King Henry I helped secure his victory.

David was a very powerful man; he was educated to a 'Norman standard' in England and, as well as being King of Scotland, he had also inherited several English titles through his marriage to a rich heiress from Northamptonshire.

David is renowned for three huge changes during his reign: the introduction of feudalism, the introduction of coinage and his monastic patronage.

David I established a feudal system through which he distributed large estates among Scottish and Anglo-Norman friends and the church. In a feudal system, the 'vassals' (or knights) to whom the king grants land must promise not to fight against the king and to give him what he asks for, be it military support, money or hospitality. The land became more and more divided with each lower order having to promise services or money in return for land. Slowly, Scotland's government and culture became more like that of the Anglo-Norman government in England.

Being a religious man, David founded many monasteries, the most famous being Holyrood Abbey and Melrose Abbey. However, these had more than a religious function – they became places of political and

ALEXANDER'S COIN
Scottish coin depicting Alexander I.

MELROSE ABBEY
Founded by David I in 1136.

foreign influence and a place for literate men to shape future politics. The labour provided by the monasteries also boosted Scotland's economy.

BURGHS

David I is responsible for creating the first burghs (or towns) of Scotland. A burgh was a settlement with defined boundaries and trading rules. The king would collect taxes from each burgh. The first burgh was Berwick-upon-Tweed, followed by Roxburgh, Stirling, Aberdeen, Scone and Edinburgh – he created 15 burghs in total. The word 'burgh' is derived from the old English word 'burh', which had the same meaning and has since evolved into the modern word 'borough'. The Scottish burghs were heavily influenced by Anglo-Norman culture, and the rise of the Scots language, which developed from Old English, led to the undermining of Gaelic.

David I

Alexander II came to the throne in 1214 and was the first king to control almost all of Scotland. Thanks to his diplomatic help in the battle between the French and the English for the crown of England, and his marriage to King Henry III's sister, Joan, he placed himself in a strong political position, becoming the only Scottish king to take an army as far as the south coast of England. Alexander also attempted to reconquer Northumbria, but several treaties and the reluctance of the English barons to fight, led to peace being declared at Newcastle. This was formalised in the Treaty of York, signed in 1237, which officially defined the border between England and Scotland.

DUFFUS CASTLE, NEAR ELGIN
The keep, seen here, was destroyed during David I's reign.

Alexander then looked to the west to extend the kingdom. The Lords of the Hebrides and Argyll still swore allegiance to the kings of Norway. Alexander made several unsuccessful attempts to buy that allegiance. When he died, he passed on his ambitions for expanding the kingdom to his son, Alexander III.

ALEXANDER III
Finished what his father had started, defeating the King of Norway in 1263 to end the Norse threat in the Hebrides and Argyll.

The Great Cause

Alexander III died with no direct successor to the throne. The business of selecting a new king became known as the 'Great Cause'.

KING JOHN BALLIOL
Was inaugurated in 1292, but his reign would not last long.

A total of 13 claimants to the throne came forward; the two strongest were John Balliol and Robert de Brus (the grandfather of King Robert the Bruce). Both men were descended from David I's youngest son and Balliol was also the son of Dervorguilla, a Gael. As the two contenders struggled for power, Scotland came under greater threat of civil war. The Scottish nobles turned to King Edward I of England to decide. Edward had initially been invited to keep the peace by bishops concerned about civil war.

Edward ruthlessly exploited his position to undermine the Kingdom of Scotland, demanding that only claimants who accept him as overlord of Scotland would be considered. Both claimants to the throne agreed, but it was Balliol whom Edward chose, as Balliol had a stronger legal claim to the throne.

John Balliol was inaugurated in 1292 and, almost immediately, the English king made his terms clear. He demanded that Balliol pay homage to him and that the Scots fight for the English against the French, as well as contribute to the English defence costs.

Edward's demands, however, proved a step too far for Balliol and he forged an alliance with the French, agreeing to support them if the English attacked them. This became known as the Auld Alliance.

Some historians believe that Edward knew Balliol would do this all along; by pushing Balliol towards the French he had created a reason to invade Scotland. Balliol's defiance marked the beginning of the Wars of Independence.

The Scots attacked Carlisle and Edward quickly sent his army north, quashing the Scots. He then went on to Berwick, where his army slaughtered almost every inhabitant of the town. Many of the Scottish nobles who owned estates in England under

EDWARD I
Used his position to force any claimant to the Scottish throne to accept him as overlord.

the feudal system surrendered and paid homage to Edward I, including Robert de Brus. Balliol was enraged and gave de Brus' land to his brother-in-law, John 'the Red' de Comyn.

Edward, together with some Scottish nobles, marched to Dunbar, where he defeated the Scottish army and stripped Balliol of the crown. Edward continued his progress through Scotland, forcing all Scottish nobles to sign the 'Ragman's Roll', a contract that recognised Edward as their king.

DIRLETON CASTLE
Near North Berwick. John Balliol was ordered by Edward I to relinquish control of castles in Berwick, Roxburgh and Jedburgh.

THE STONE OF SCONE

Edward took back to England with him the Stone of Scone, the symbol of Scottish kingship. He had the stone built into a special coronation chair at Westminster Abbey. This chair is often referred to as 'St Edward's Chair' or 'The Coronation Chair'. The stone was a symbol of England's supremacy over Scotland and remained in England for seven centuries, housed in the chair in which most subsequent English monarchs were crowned. The stone was given back to Scotland in 1996 and is now housed with the Crown Jewels of Scotland at Edinburgh Castle.

EDWARD I'S FLEET
Sailed north to Newcastle, where his tenants were made to fight against the 'rebelling' Scots.

William Wallace

William Wallace, who is also known as Braveheart, fought to free Scotland from English rule.

BRAVEHEART
The statue of William Wallace at Edinburgh Castle.

Wallace was already considered an outlaw by 1297. He had allegedly been visiting a woman, believed by some to have been his wife, in Lanark. He became involved in a fight with English soldiers and the girl, Marion, had helped him escape. Wallace escaped, but the girl was captured and put to death by the English sheriff. Wallace was infuriated and returned under cover of night to kill the sheriff. Legend has it he stabbed him to death in his bed while he slept. When news of Wallace's act spread, he soon became the figurehead of a national resistance movement.

The English reacted to the growing resistance by marching a large, over-confident army to Stirling Bridge. King Edward's army was obliterated by a Scottish force led by William Wallace and his fellow rebel, Andrew Moray. The English retreated to Berwick.

HOW WALLACE WON STIRLING BRIDGE

Aside from poor communication on the English side, Wallace and Moray's victory over the English was impressive not only because they lacked the cavalry and weaponry of the English, but because many of their soldiers were peasants and common folk.

The key to winning was the schiltron. A schiltron was a huge circular formation of men who carried long spears that pointed outwards. The schiltron lines were tightly packed and proved almost impenetrable, and deadly, to English mounted knights.

Stirling Bridge

Wallace became Guardian of Scotland and went very quickly from underground guerrilla warrior to leader of southern Scotland and its armies. Wallace's overwhelming victory at Stirling Bridge angered Edward I and he turned all of his attention, and that of his loyal English nobles, to the problem of the Scots, which culminated in the battle of Falkirk.

Once again the Scots were massively outnumbered and lacked the heavy weaponry and cavalry of the English. Wallace's men formed huge schiltrons, as they

WALLACE MEMORIAL
At St Bartholomew's Hospital, London.

WALLACE MONUMENT
Overlooking the scene
of Scotland's victory
at Stirling Bridge.

had in the Battle of Stirling Bridge, and were backed up by bowmen inside the schiltrons and mounted knights behind the front line.

At first, English advances failed and mounted knights were impaled on the spears of the Scots. However, for unknown reasons, the Scots nobles fled the battlefield. This gave the English knights new confidence and they attacked the Scottish bowmen. Edward had a further trick up his sleeve: English longbowmen who fired iron-tipped arrows that caused fatal damage and broke the impenetrable lines of the Scottish schiltrons.

The Scots fled to the woods as the English knights began to cut through the Scottish warriors. Wallace escaped and resigned as Guardian of Scotland. He was eventually captured in 1305 and tried for murder and treason. Wallace's defence was that it was impossible for him to be guilty of treason against the king since he'd never sworn allegiance to King Edward. He was found guilty and was dragged through the streets, then he was hanged, but taken down before he died; he was disembowelled, beheaded and cut into four pieces. The four quarters of his body were taken to Berwick, Newcastle, Stirling and Perth and put on display as an example to other rebels. His head was impaled and displayed above London Bridge.

BATTLE OF FALKIRK
The Scots were outnumbered and suffered heavy defeat at the hands of King Edward's army.

Wallace became a national hero with legendary status, and tales of his heroic battles and defiance of the English were passed down through the generations – the most famous being the account of his story by the 15th-century poet, Blind Harry.

ROBERT THE BRUCE
One of Scotland's
most famous kings.

King Robert the Bruce

Robert de Brus, often called Robert the Bruce, is widely regarded as one of Scotland's great kings and fighters.

Robert the Bruce was the grandson of Robert de Brus, who lost his claim to the Scottish throne to John Balliol. The Bruces did not support Balliol's reign and instead chose to pay homage to the English king, Edward I. This angered Balliol and he gave the Bruce's Scottish land to his brother-in-law, John 'the Red' de Comyn.

When Balliol was stripped of the crown for defying Edward I, the first Wars of Independence broke out. After the execution of William Wallace, both Comyn and Bruce became Guardians of Scotland. After the death of his father, Bruce believed he should claim back the Scottish throne. He appeared to arrange a meeting with Comyn to discuss his terms and, when they met, he stabbed Comyn. Events prior to this fight are not known; however, the pope excommunicated Bruce for this heinous act.

The bishops of Scotland were a strong political force at that time and knew there would be danger of civil war without a clear successor to the 'throne'. Outwardly they supported the exiled Balliol, but were, most likely, secretly in favour of Bruce.

Bruce was crowned King of Scots at Scone. Edward I was once again angered by Scotland's disobedience and sent an army north. He easily crushed Bruce's men and, in retaliation for the Scottish 'uprising' he captured Bruce's wife, daughters and sisters and imprisoned them in London; Bruce's brothers were executed for treason. Meanwhile, Bruce fled Scotland.

Many historians disagree about where exactly Robert the Bruce spent his time in exile. However, most believe he took refuge in the Western Isles and the islands off the east coast of Ireland. There are many myths and legends about this period of his life – the most famous is about him seeking refuge in a cave and watching a spider trying to swing itself from its thin, silvery thread. Robert had tried and

JOHN THE RED COMYN
Acted as Guardian of Scotland with Bruce.

BRUCE'S MARRIAGE
To Elizabeth De Burgh, the Earl of Ulster's daughter.

AND EFTER KING ROBERT YE BRVCE MARIIT YE DVKE OF HVLLISTERIS DOCHTER

failed to defeat the English six times; as he watched the spider persevere, he thought, 'If the spider fails again, I will give up too.' But the spider swung with all its might and, on the seventh attempt, it swung to the beam it had been trying to reach. This perseverance inspired Bruce to return to Scotland and fight the English once again.

Bruce returned to Scotland and started a guerrilla war, much as Braveheart had done before him. He defeated Edward's men at Glen Trool and then went on to fight and reclaim land from his Scottish enemies, including many Comyn-owned areas. Bruce's men tore through the land, reclaiming and then destroying castles, so

RATHLIN ISLAND
Where Robert most likely took refuge in 1307.

RIVER TAY
By 1309 Robert the Bruce controlled all of Scotland north of the River Tay.

that any invading English army would struggle for shelter and resources.

King Edward I died and was succeeded by his son, Edward II. Edward II marched his men towards Stirling Castle, which Bruce had demanded the English give up. The two sides met at the Battle of Bannockburn, where the Scots defeated the English at the cost of thousands of lives. Bruce captured English noblemen and used them to trade back his family. Bruce continued to push back the English, taking the final English stronghold, Berwick, in 1318. However, Edward still claimed to be 'overlord' of Scotland.

Nearly 10 years later Edward II was murdered as a result of English royal rivalry and the English finally made peace with Scotland, renouncing their 'overlordship'. This meant that Scotland was an independent nation once again.

DUNFERMLINE ABBEY
Houses the tomb of Robert the Bruce.

The Battle of Bannockburn

The Battle of Bannockburn took place in June 1314 and was one of the most significant victories in the Scottish Wars of Independence.

After returning from exile, Bruce won some small guerrilla battles and ousted many Scottish nobles who had supported Balliol. These nobles joined forced with Edward II to get Balliol, and their lands, back. Bruce had lost many friends in battle and his family had either been killed or were imprisoned in England.

But when the new King Edward II marched a huge army towards Stirling Castle, Bruce faced him head on. They chose the battleground of Bannockburn and prepared the ground before the English arrived. The Scots were heavily outnumbered by at least three to one, with the English having over 2,000 mounted knights compared to the Scots' 500.

But the Scots had learned from previous defeats and dug pit traps on each side of the battleground so that the English couldn't outflank them and would have to face them head on.

BATTLE OF BANNOCKBURN
Where the Scots defeated the English at the cost of thousands of lives.

On the first day, the Scots formed huge schiltrons that proved almost impenetrable to the English knights. Famously, Bruce, armed only with a battle axe and riding a small horse, still managed to slay an English knight, Henry de Bohun, who charged at him. On the second day, Edward II made an ill-fated decision, ordering his troops to cross the river where they got caught in boggy ground – the Scots attacked in formation with devastating effect. The English struggled to retreat across the river, with many mounted knights trampling foot soldiers in their wake. The Scots continued to push back the English – many legends tell of the river filling with the bodies of English soldiers.

Edward II escaped the battlefield and fled to Dunbar Castle, where he took a boat back to England. Many English who fled south were pursued by Scottish warriors or were even

DUNBAR CASTLE
Where Edward retreated and boarded a ship to England.

killed by local residents as they passed through Scottish villages.

The Scots used captured English nobles as leverage to ransom Bruce's family, who had been imprisoned since he first claimed the throne in 1306.

ROBERT THE BRUCE
This statue at Bannockburn commemorates Bruce's victory.

Scottish victory at Bannockburn strengthened Bruce's position in Scotland and effectively ended English control. Bruce continued south, eventually taking back the royal burgh of Berwick from the English, but despite overwhelming Scottish victories and almost no English authority in Scotland, Edward II still claimed to be 'overlord'. Bruce continued his campaign, opening a new front in Ireland, but it wasn't until 1327, during the reign of King Edward III, that a truce was called and Scotland's independence was recognised by both Edward and the pope.

The Bannockburn Heritage Centre, run by the National Trust for Scotland, is open to the public. It is situated near Borestone – the command post used by Bruce during the battle.

The Stuarts Arrive

The Stuart dynasty really began with Robert II in 1371 and finally ended with the death of Anne of Great Britain in 1714.

JAMES I
Became King of
Scotland in 1424.

The dynasty became synonymous with Scotland. The Stuart clan developed Scotland from a poor, feudal country into a modern and economically prosperous state and their reign saw the transition from the middle ages through to the Renaissance period and beyond.

The first James became King of Scots in 1424. Before becoming king he had been detained in England, where he was educated. He developed a great respect for the English, to such an extent that he even fought for King Henry V against the Scots in France. Although James was next in line to the throne of Scotland, James' cousin, Murdoch, Duke of Albany was awarded governorship over the country in his absence. As a result, the powerful Albany Stuarts did little to secure James' release, perhaps hoping that Murdoch would take the throne instead.

A £40,000 ransom was eventually paid for James and he returned to Scotland, where he initiated attacks on those he considered rivals, including the Albany Stuarts, and killed Duke Murdoch. At this time, Scotland was in an economic recession. Instead of continuing to pay the ransom debts owed, James spent lavishly on Linlithgow Palace and on luxuries for his court. During his reign, Scotland's first university, the University of St Andrews, was founded. His irresponsible spending angered the Scottish nobles and he was assassinated in a monastery in Perth in 1437.

James I's son, James II, was only a boy when he became king in 1437; he was crowned at Holyrood Abbey, the first Scottish king not to be crowned at Scone. During his minority, rival families fought for control, culminating in the so-called 'Black Dinner' at Edinburgh Castle, when the Earl of Douglas was executed. Once in full control, James II reorganised central government and quashed warring factions, most notably the Douglases, a powerful dynasty who tried to conspire against King James II to claim

JAMES II
Led unsuccessful attempts to regain the Orkney Islands and the Isle of Man for Scotland.

JAMES III
Became King of
Scotland in 1460.

JAMES IV
King of Scots
from 1488–1513.

the throne for themselves. During his reign, James II built on his father's love of literature and learning by founding the University of Glasgow in 1451. He reorganised government and taxes and, rather strangely, banned the sports of golf and football – encouraging men to practise archery instead.

James acquired cannons from Burgundy and set about attacking Roxburgh Castle, which was still held by the English following the Wars of Independence. Unfortunately, he stood too close to a cannon and was killed by exploding shrapnel. He was succeeded by his son, James III.

King James III of Scotland proved a rather unsuccessful monarch, although he did succeed in gaining back the Orkney and Shetland Isles from Denmark as part of a dowry for his wife, Margaret of Denmark. He was rumoured to have been bisexual and preferred music and literature to hunting and war.

James III had ambitious plans for extending the Scottish kingdom, but failed attempts at alliance and then war with England undermined his reign.

He faced challenges to the throne, first from the Boyds of Kilmarnock and then from his brothers, Alexander of Albany and John, Earl of Mar. James angered his nobles further by granting an earldom to a man considered to be his low-born favourite. He was killed during the Battle of Sauchieburn and succeeded by his son, James IV.

James IV is considered to be the first real Renaissance king, greatly influenced by the Renaissance movement in Europe. He spoke many languages and encouraged the arts and learning. He founded Aberdeen University and the Royal College of Surgeons in Edinburgh. James also made education compulsory for all nobility and successfully quashed the MacDonald hold over the Hebrides. His marriage to the daughter of Henry VII of England would eventually bring the thrones of Scotland and England together in the person of James VI.

ROYAL COLLEGE OF SURGEONS
Founded by James IV in 1506.

The Lords of the Isles

This title goes back to the first settlers of the Scottish Isles, which included the Hebrides, the Western Isles and the Isle of Man.

MACDONALD CLAN
Successfully contested the title of Lord of the Isles.

After a series of both Viking and Gaelic invasions, a hierarchy of island chiefs emerged and functioned independently of the Scottish crown. Their territories were the Hebrides and the Kintyre peninsula.

The Lords of the Isles wielded great power because of the strategic position of the Isles for both war and trade. The lords' knowledge of longships, probably learnt from Vikings, made them a powerful maritime force and they often took part in sea battles and attacked castles close to the sea.

The MacDonald clan was a powerful dynasty that contested territory with the MacDougal clan. The Scottish Isles had been 'owned' by Norway since the Viking invasions, and in the 13th century King Haakon IV of Norway decreed that Angus MacDonald would be the first Lord of Islay (an island in the

Hebrides). MacDonald fought for Norway at the Battle of Largs, which ended in Scottish victory. He later made a deal with King Alexander III, agreeing to him as 'overlord' if he could retain his land.

The MacDonalds were keen to strengthen their control over the Isles and, having supported Robert the Bruce during the Wars of Independence, they were granted more land, which included the Isles of Skye and Lewis, as well as mainland territories in Glencoe and Lochaber.

ISLE OF CARA
The only island with direct MacDonald descendants.

EILEAN MÓR

The island located on Loch Finlaggen, situated inside the island of Islay, formed the administrative centre of the Isles and is where the distinctly separate clans gradually swore their allegiance to the MacDonalds.

Finlaggen Castle – where the Council of the Isles met.

HEBRIDES
The Hebrides and the Kintyre penninsula formed the Lordship of the Isles.

The MacDonalds' system of control was based on kin alliance, physical power and the Council of the Isles; they set their sights on further territories in Scotland and the clan was regarded as a power to be reckoned with.

The Stuart dynasty was in power at this time and the mighty MacDonalds made secret deals with the English and the exiled Douglases to rip apart Scotland to regain land and power. However, the plans were leaked and John MacDonald was later stripped of his land, title and influence by King James III. John MacDonald's son was angered by the humiliation to the clan, blaming clan members for the leak; disputes escalated into a bloody civil war, culminating in the self-destruction of the MacDonald clan near the coast of Mull.

King James IV of Scotland sent a fleet to the Isles and the Lords of the Isles and their powerful legacy came to an abrupt end. The title Lord of the Isles is still in existence as a ceremonial title that is given to the eldest male child of the reigning Scottish (and now British) monarch.

The only island that remains in possession of the direct descendants of the Norse-Gaelic Lords of the Isles is the island of Cara, off Kintyre. The island is owned by the MacDonalds of Largie, and is the only territory left of what was once an expansive heritage.

GALLEY BOATS
Based on a Viking longboat design, they were used by the inhabitants of the Isles, who had learned naval tactics from their Viking ancestors.

Stirling Castle

Having played a central role throughout the country's history, Stirling Castle is one of Scotland's most important castles.

STIRLING CASTLE
Has a strong
defensive position
on steep cliffs.

The castle is likely to have been built around the time of Alexander I in the early 12th century. Stirling became a royal burgh and a popular royal residence over the next hundred years. During John Balliol's reign, King Edward I attacked Scotland and found the castle abandoned. It remained an English stronghold until the Battle of Stirling Bridge, when William Wallace (Braveheart) and Andrew Moray took it back. During the Wars of Independence the castle changed hands between the English and the Scots until

Robert the Bruce defeated the English forces at the Battle of Bannockburn in 1314 and the castle once again came back to the Scots.

ROBERT THE BRUCE
One of Stirling Castle's most famous statues.

The Stuart dynasty built Stirling Castle into the structure it is today. The Stuart kings, heavily influenced by the Renaissance, embarked on an ambitious building programme that lasted from the reign of Robert III to that of James V. James V's daughter, Mary, Queen of Scots, was later crowned at Stirling Castle. This was a tumultuous time for the Scots and fortifications were added to its south side. The castle served not only as a royal residence, but as a chapel, school and a place of learning for Scottish nobility. During this period, the castle played an important role in the Renaissance movement sweeping through Scotland.

During the 17th century, Stirling Castle became less important as a royal residence and served as a

military centre. The castle came under attack during the British Civil Wars and the damage can still be seen today in the chapel and the great hall.

The castle later played an important role during the Jacobite Risings, coming under attack after the Jacobites retreated from England.

JAMES V OF SCOTLAND
Continued and expanded his father's building programme at Stirling Castle.

Many parts of the castle have been restored and the project is still ongoing today. The castle has a much more peaceful role as a concert venue and as a set for several films, as well as hosting many celebrations. It is the second most popular visitor attraction in Scotland and is open to the public all year round.

STIRLING CASTLE
Had become a great Renaissance palace by the mid-16th century.

The Makars

The Makars were the first famous Scottish writers and included John Barbour, Robert Henryson, William Dunbar, Gavin Douglas and David Lyndsay.

Makars were originally poets of the royal court. As the Renaissance influence spread and knowledge of other languages and literature became available to nobility, skilful poets came on the court scene. James I encouraged the existing tradition of poetry as a central part of court culture and the poetic tradition grew, first through court poets and then throughout the nobility and educated Scots.

John Barbour was the first recognised Scottish poet and is most famous for his work, *The Brus* (c. 1370), an epic poem about Robert the Bruce. Barbour served in the court of the first Stuart king, Robert II, and although print hadn't been invented at this time, some of Barbour's works survived; the most famous lines from *The Brus* are often quoted as a symbol of Scottish literary tradition:

Ah! Fredome is a noble thing!
Fredome mays man to haiff liking;
Fredome all solace to man giffis:
He levys at es that frely levys!
And suld think fredome mar to prys,
Than all the gold in warld that is.

Robert Henryson was writing during the 15th century and is regarded as one of the finest poets in the Scots language. Like Barbour, his work was mostly secular and told a story about everyday life situations. His most famous work is the extremely long poem, *Morall Fabillis* (moral fable), which appears to question the ruling power of the church.

William Dunbar was a contemporary of Henryson and may have served in the court of James IV, for which he would have received a salary. His poem, *The Goldyn Targe*, was one of the first books to be printed in Scotland. The printing press came to Scotland from France, where Scottish

THE GOLDYN TARGE
The frontispiece of one of the first books to be printed in Scotland.

GAVIN DOUGLAS
His statue can
be seen at St
Giles Cathedral,
Edinburgh.

authors had previously travelled to get their books printed before a licence to print in Scotland was granted by King James IV.

Dunbar was considered one of the great Scottish poets and evidence suggests that his work influenced many of his contemporaries and, years later, Scotland's most famous poet, Robert Burns.

> *Our pleasance here is all vain glory,*
> *This false world is but transitory;*
> *The flesh is bruckle, the Fiend is slee:–*
> *Timor Mortis conturbat me.*

Dunbar, 'Lament for the Makaris', 1505.

Gavin Douglas was a bishop and, despite an influential political career, he is best remembered for his poetry. His most important work was the translation of Virgil's *Aeneid* into Scots. His original work, *The Palice of Honour* (1500–01), is his earliest and best-known work; it tells the story of a poet's adventures in the courts of Venus. Because of his social standing, Douglas's life is one of the best documented of the Scottish Makars.

Sir David Lyndsay's poetry was heavily influenced by the Renaissance movement and, like all Makar poets, by the 14th-century English writer, Geoffrey Chaucer. Lyndsay's work captured the essence of the time, questioning the world around him and the ruling power of the church.

SIR DAVID LYNDSAY
His work was heavily influenced by the English writer, Chaucer.

> *Unthrift, sweirnes, falset, povertie, and stryfe*
> *Pat polacey in dainger of hir lyfe.*

Lyndsay, 'The Dreme', c. 1528.

The Makars played an important role in Scottish literary history and paved the way for a great tradition of poets that would come after them. Their rise in popularity and influence can be attributed to the Stuart kings and the spread of Renaissance ideas.

The Reformation

The Scottish reformation took place in the mid-16th century and signalled a break from Catholicism and the Pope.

The Scottish reformation had been coming since the Renaissance movement of the 15th century, which had encouraged critical thinking about the church and theological ideas. The reformation was also symbolic of a political battle between France and England, with the English Protestant influence eventually triumphing over French Catholicism.

MARTIN LUTHER
Martin Luther's ideas were influential in Scotland.

Luther, a German monk who played a pivotal role in the European Protestant Reformation, first introduced the idea of reformation. The then Catholic Scottish government saw Luther's ideas as a threat and banned his books; however, this proved quite unsuccessful as a deterrent to his supporters.

By 1535, England's King Henry VIII had broken ties with the Vatican and created the Protestant Church of England. At this point, Scotland was still very much

Catholic and had carried out public executions of Protestant teachers and sympathisers. They passed legislation to protect the celebration of mass and the offering of prayers to the Virgin Mary, and still abided by the Pope's authority. But Protestant ideas were attracting increasing attention, with many leaning towards a new alliance with the English over the centuries-old Auld Alliance with the French.

At this time, Mary I of Scotland, James V's daughter, became queen. Mary became involved in a political struggle for Scotland between the French and the English. She was originally promised in marriage to Henry VIII's son, the future King Edward VI, but her Catholic mother, Marie de Guise, strongly opposed the match. She fled with her daughter to France, where Mary was married to Dauphin Francis, son of the French King.

In 1546, George Wishart, a Protestant preacher, was burned at the stake on the instructions of Cardinal Beaton. Protestant supporters plotted their revenge on the cardinal and murdered him in his castle at St

QUEEN ELIZABETH I
Promoted Protestantism in England and Scotland.

MARIE DE GUISE
Sought to punish Protestant rebels.

Andrews. Marie de Guise, who was acting as regent until her daughter Mary came of age, sent a French army to capture the plotters, who were subjected to torture and slavery. One of the Protestants captured was John Knox.

John Knox soon became a figurehead of the Protestant reformation. In 1559 he returned to Scotland, following his escape from a French slave ship. He travelled the country, preaching against Catholicism. He directed much of his anger towards the young Mary, Queen of Scots, publishing his opinions in *The First Blast of the Trumpet Against The Monstrous Regimen of Women*.

FRIARS EVICTED
During the Protestant reformation.

Although his writings were directed at Mary I and her mother, his misogynistic message did not go down well with the new Queen of England, Elizabeth I, who never forgave him.

Inspired by Knox, a Protestant movement spearheaded by the Lords of Congregation marched through Scotland attacking Catholic churches. This eventually led to a battle between the Lords, who had support from the English, and Marie de Guise's French troops. Marie de Guise died only months after the war had started and a peace treaty was signed between English and French troops. Marie's death allowed the Lords of Congregation to gain control of the Scottish parliament. They immediately renounced their allegiance to the Pope and banned any form of Catholic mass in Scotland. This was the beginning of Protestantism in Scotland and the origin of the Church of Scotland.

JOHN KNOX
Spearheaded the Protestant reformation.

MARY STUART
The young Queen
of France and
Scotland.

Mary, Queen of Scots

The young monarch could have been Queen of France, England and Scotland, but her personal life led to her downfall.

Mary was born in 1542 just six days before the death of her father, James V of Scotland. Her mother, Marie de Guise, acted as regent. At the age of just six months, Mary was betrothed to the future King Edward VI of England. However, the Scots were not happy with the terms of Mary's betrothal, as it meant breaking Scotland's Auld Alliance with France.

ROUGH WOOING

Soon after Mary was crowned, the Scots broke their agreement to the English marriage proposal. Henry VIII was furious and attacked Scotland with extreme force with the aim of intimidating the Scots into agreeing to the marriage. Henry's forces terrorised the Scots for two years and, following his death in 1547, his son, Edward VI, continued to bombard them. This came to a head at the Battle of Pinkie Cleugh on 10 September 1547; the Scots were bombarded by English artillery and naval ships and the day became known as 'Black Saturday'. Marie de Guise still would not give up her daughter and instead took her to France, to the French court.

Once in France, Mary became the subject of a new treaty between the Scots and the French, under which she was betrothed to the French crown prince, Dauphin Francis. Mary grew up in France a devout Catholic and learnt many languages. At the age of 15 she married Francis. A year later, in 1559, King Henry II of France died and was succeeded by Francis, and Mary was now Queen of France and Scotland.

Tragically, King Francis II died just one year later in 1560 and Mary's mother died later that same year. Francis' brother took the throne and a devastated Mary, widowed at 17, returned to Scotland.

Although there was much celebration upon her return, Mary was the Catholic queen of what had officially become a Protestant country. She returned to a turbulent political situation: England and France had been warring over Scotland, with the Protestant Lords of Congregation campaigning against Marie de Guise's rule in Scotland. After her mother's death a peace was brokered and Mary returned to Scotland as queen, with a Protestant government.

DAUPHIN FRANCIS
Mary's husband and Prince of France.

HENRY VIII
Was furious when Mary did not marry his son, Edward.

Some dogmatic Protestant Scots were quick to criticise Mary's Catholic practices and protested outside her residence at Holyrood House.

She needed to provide an heir to the throne, something Elizabeth I had failed to do and as a result, the clock was ticking down to the end of the Tudor dynasty. Because a Catholic marriage would have angered the English and possibly provoked war, in the end she married Lord Darnley, a distant relative of royal lineage.

COAT OF ARMS
Used by Mary when she was Queen of Scotland and France.

The match seemed like a good choice; Mary adored Lord Darnley and their children would have a claim to both the Scottish and English thrones. However, Darnley turned out to be disreputable and spent many nights in taverns and brothels. In 1566 his behaviour took a disastrous turn, when, encouraged by Protestant noblemen, he planned to murder the Queen's courtier and private secretary, David Rizzio, believing him to have been having an affair with his wife. Darnley's aides kidnapped Rizzio in front of the Queen, dragged him away and stabbed him to death.

A year later Darnley was blown up in mysterious circumstances and Mary went on to marry the prime suspect, James Hepburn, Earl of Bothwell. This provoked uproar among her Protestant enemies who tricked Mary into abdicating the throne. Mary's supporters helped her escape from her prison at Lochleven Island, where she immediately reclaimed the throne and raised an army.

Mary suffered a terrible defeat at the Battle of Langside and, in desperation, she turned to her cousin, Elizabeth I of England. Instead of helping her, Elizabeth held her captive in England for 18 years. She was tried for the murder of her second husband but her involvement could not be proved. The English, believing her to be too dangerous to be allowed to return to Scotland, kept her imprisoned for many years. She was implicated in a fabricated Catholic plot against Elizabeth and was executed at Fotheringay Castle on 8 February 1587.

EXECUTION
Mary was executed at Fotheringay Castle in Northamptonshire.

The Clever King James VI

James was the first King of Scotland to become King of England and Ireland, due to his royal lineage on both sides of the border.

GEORGE VILLIERS
Some historians claim he was one of James's lovers.

Born in 1566, James was the son of Mary, Queen of Scots, and became King of Scotland at the age of only 13 months, when Mary was forced to abdicate. Although baptised a Catholic, James was raised as a Protestant. He finally took control of his Scottish kingdom in 1581, at the age of 15.

Although James was married to Anne of Denmark in 1589, he was known to have close friendships with several of his male courtiers, which has led many historians to speculate about the true nature of those relationships. Many believe Esmé Stewart, the Duke of Lennox, to have been his first lover, followed by Robert Carr and, later, George Villiers. In fact, restoration of James VI's residence, Apethorpe Hall, has revealed a secret passage linking the bedrooms of King James and George Villiers.

James was a superstitious king who feared witchcraft; he was a key figure in the North Berwick witch trials of 1590 and was the author of *Daemonologie*, a book that spoke about the dangers of witches and the devil. However, evidence suggests in later life that he became less convinced of the existence of witchcraft.

RUTHVEN CASTLE
Where James was imprisoned and forced to denounce Esmé Stewart, Duke of Lennox.

In 1603, James succeeded Elizabeth I to the English throne, the first monarch to have had a legitimate claim to both the English and Scottish thrones. However, the two countries remained individual sovereign states at this time. James wanted to establish a single country under one monarch, but was met with heavy opposition from both the English and the Scots.

THE GUNPOWDER PLOT

Led by the Catholic activist, Guy Fawkes, the plot involved the murder of King James, his family, parliament and all the Protestant nobility, in the hope of initiating a Catholic uprising. Guy Fawkes had discovered a cellar beneath the Houses of Parliament and, along with 13 conspirators, he planted 36 barrels of gunpowder there. One conspirator, Francis Tresham, wrote a letter to his friend in parliament, Lord Monteagle, warning him to stay away. Monteagle took the letter to Secretary of State Robert Cecil, and the plotters were caught and executed. Guy Fawkes was caught red-handed on 4 November 1605, setting the gunpowder for the opening of parliament the following day. The Gunpowder Plot is remembered in the UK every 5 November, when giant effigies of Guy Fawkes are burned and firework displays are put on.

The proposal became known as the Union of the Crown.

James, like his predecessor Elizabeth, became a patron of Shakespeare and Shakespeare's troupe of actors was renamed 'The King's Men'. Shakespeare's tragedy, *Macbeth*, the 'Scottish play', featured three witches, a subject about which Shakespeare knew James was passionate.

The colonisation of America began under James's rule, with Jamestown in Virginia becoming the first English settlement there in 1606. Virginia's main export was tobacco and this trade with England forged an important trading relationship. However, James detested smoking and gave what has since proved to be the prophetic warning that it was 'loathsome to the eye, hateful to the nose, harmful to the brain and dangerous to the lungs'.

James I is also remembered for authorising the official translation of the Bible into English. The King James Bible is still used widely today.

JAMES VI
The first King of both Scotland and England.

KING JAMES BIBLE
The first official Bible in English.

The Border Reivers

The Border Reivers, or Borderers, were English and Scottish families who raided both sides of the Anglo-Scottish border with impartiality.

The borderlands had been devastated time and time again during the many wars between Scotland and England, with neither country helping the border inhabitants to rebuild their communities. Furthermore, the mountainous nature of the land meant that farming was largely unsuccessful. The Border Reivers received mixed messages from both

English and Scottish governments; during times of war or uncertainty their actions were almost encouraged, as they would act as the first line of defence on a threatened border. However, during peacetime, their actions were condemned and punishments for their criminal activities were severe. This undermined their already fragile infrastructure and forced them to continue raiding.

Border Reivers were skilled soldiers and considered to be the finest light cavalry in Europe. However, when forced to fight in battle, they switched sides at will and raided and plundered for their own benefit. Intermarriage across the border meant that the Reivers could choose their nationality, depending on circumstances, and they were even known to change sides mid-battle.

RUINED BASTLE HOUSE
Bastle houses inhabited by borderers had elaborate defensive measures to prevent counter-raids.

The border-dwellers often lived in constant fear of attack. They lived in peel towers or on the top floor of bastle houses, accessible only by an external ladder that could be pulled up in times of danger.

SMAILHOLM TOWER
The only surviving peel tower.

BORDER LAW

The 14th and 15th centuries saw the emergence of Border law, and a code of honour was established with rules that applied to all feuding clans. Under Border law, a person who had been raided was allowed to initiate a counter-raid. Those living nearby had to help with the counter-raid or be considered conspirators in the original raid. The areas either side of the border became split into marches and were 'ruled' by march wardens. Wardens often abused their power, ruling in favour of their own families and mounting raids on the pretext of recovering stolen goods. March wardens, who were appointed by parliament, were usually ineffective, because they couldn't command the respect of the local inhabitants.

In 1587, a new statute listed the various border clans by area and family name. The marches were split into three areas for both England and Scotland. However, the Borderers continued to fight, with the violence escalating towards the end of the 16th century.

After the death of Elizabeth I, the Borderers siezed the opportunity of uncontrolled raiding and violence. However, after the accession of James VI of Scotland to the English throne, all illegal activity on the Borders was brutally supressed and the most notorious criminals and their families were hanged without trial; some bargained for deportation or military service in return for sparing the lives of their families.

Many ballads and poems have been written about the Borderers, with the majority – most notably those by Sir Walter Scott – glorifying their activities.

HERMITAGE CASTLE
An important stronghold for border clans.

King or Covenant

In Scotland Charles I is best remembered for enforcing repressive religious control and sparking several Scottish and English civil wars.

CHARLES I
Tried to enforce religious reform in Scotland.

Charles I was the second son of James VI and, following the death of his brother, Henry, he became heir to the throne, becoming king in 1625.

Charles married a Roman Catholic and many felt he was bringing the Protestant religion too close to the Roman Catholic Church. Furthermore, he became a tyrannical leader, separating himself from parliament, in the belief that his absolute right to leadership came from God.

Charles attempted to force religious reform on the Scottish people, directly ignoring parliamentary opinion. He favoured an Episcopalian method of church government (whereby bishops had authority), whereas much of Scotland preferred a Presbyterian system that did not involve bishops. This eventually led to civil unrest and the Bishops' Wars.

In 1637, Charles forced the Book of Common Prayer on Scottish church practices. This led to riots and the formation of an opposition movement known as the National Covenant.

BOOK OF COMMON PRAYER
Was forced on Scottish churches by Charles I.

NATIONAL COVENANT

The National Covenant was an agreement signed by those Scots who took issue with Charles' forced reforms. Charles believed that, as king, he was the spiritual leader of the church. However, the Covenanters believed that no one other than Jesus could claim this right.

The Covenanters sought to protect the Protestant reformation in Scotland and put themselves at odds with the king. Charles enforced extremely repressive laws that made it a crime punishable by death to preach from anything other than his Book of Common Prayer. His repression forced the Covenanters to side with the English Parliamentarians, who rose up against Charles when he dissolved parliament – this resulted in civil war.

Although he had disbanded the English parliament to rule alone, Charles needed parliament to collect taxes and also to suppress the Covenanters' rebellion in Scotland. Parliament saw this as an opportunity to dissuade Charles from invading Scotland and to discuss their own grievances about his rule in England. Instead, Charles made deals with Irish Catholic gentry,

CIVIL WARS
Broke out due to Charles I's religious suppression.

but it wasn't enough to keep the invading Scots at bay; Charles was forced to recall parliament in 1640.

Parliament's new control worried Irish Catholics, who had supported Charles, and civil war broke out in Ireland, leading to rumours that Charles supported Irish Catholics. In 1642, Charles attempted to arrest members of parliament for treason, which quickly led to all-out war between Parliamentarians (Roundheads) and Royalists (Cavaliers). This conflict became known as the English Civil War. The Parliamentarians defeated Charles's men and demanded a constitutional monarchy. Charles refused and a second civil war broke out. This time Charles was captured and was tried and convicted of high treason. He was executed in 1649 and the monarchy was abolished. For the first time in history, Britain was known as a commonwealth and was ruled as a republic state by a Lord Protector, Oliver Cromwell.

OLIVER CROMWELL
Took command of the short-lived Commonwealth of England, Scotland and Ireland.

The Marquis of Montrose

James Graham, the Marquis of Montrose from 1612 to 1650, was a Scots nobleman and legendary Royalist commander during the English Civil War.

THE GREAT MONTROSE
Was first a Covenanter and then a Royalist.

Montrose, however, started the campaign as a Covenanter and fought alongside the Parliamentarians, switching allegiance later on. He is often referred to in Scotland as 'The Great Montrose'.

In 1638, after Charles I had forcibly imposed his Anglican Book of Common Prayer in Scotland, many Scots rose up in rebellion, which resulted in what was known as the Bishops' Wars. Although he wasn't a particularly religious man for that time, Graham was more offended by the authority given by Charles to the bishops and was wary of their political control. Following several bloody battles, Graham visited Charles with the idealistic view of removing the church from political matters.

Even though Charles refused to annul the bishops' authority, Graham became disillusioned with the Covenanters, as he believed that they wanted the church to have complete control over Scotland. He believed that churches should concern themselves only with religious matters, while the monarch should rule the country and preserve the law.

ST ANDREWS
Montrose learnt to question religion and politics at St Andrews University.

From this point on, Montrose played a double role, leading Royalist forces against the Covenanters he had once sided with. He used his knowledge of Highland clans, Episcopalians and Irish Catholics to defeat his opponents in several early battles. In 1645, Montrose sealed his victory at the Battle of Kilsyth and the king appointed him Lord Lieutenant and Master of Scotland.

Montrose planned to call a parliament, swear allegiance to the king and separate the church from politics. However, Charles I had been defeated at

Naseby and the Highlanders had given up on the cause. Montrose fled for Norway, and Scotland, England and Ireland became part of a new republic without a monarch.

After the restoration of the monarchy, Charles' exiled son, Charles II, became king and Montrose returned to show his support. Charles II restored him as Lord Lieutenant, but Montrose had lost the support of the Highlanders, and while he travelled Europe enlisting support for the king, Charles had reopened negotiations with the Covenanters. He sent a letter to Montrose telling him to disarm, but the letter never reached him and he faced the Covenanters, now a strong force, once again. Montrose was easily defeated at the Battle of Carbisdale in 1650, in the aftermath of which Charles II disavowed him under a new treaty – the Treaty of Breda.

Montrose fled to the mountains but was betrayed and captured. He was taken to Edinburgh where he was hanged. His body was cut into pieces

ARCHIBALD CAMPBELL
Marquis of Argyll –
Montrose's opposition
after he became
a Royalist.

and distributed around the country's main towns. Eleven years later, the Scottish Argyll government had also switched sides to become Royalists. The pieces of Montrose's body were reassembled in Edinburgh and he was given a lavish funeral at St Giles' Cathedral.

ST GILES' CATHEDRAL
Montrose's severed head was displayed in front of St Giles' Cathedral in Edinburgh from 1650–61.

ARDVRECK CASTLE
Remains of Ardvreck Castle on the shores of Loch Assynt, where Montrose surrendered to Neil MacLeod.

Cromwellian Conquest

Cromwell led a cruel fight against the Scots, who did not accept the new Commonwealth but pledged their allegiance to the king's son.

Cromwell led Parliamentary troops during the English Civil War and, on signing Charles I's death warrant, became the first (and only) Lord Protector of the Commonwealth. England, Scotland and Ireland became known as a new republic state without a monarch.

The Scots, however, proclaimed Charles II as their king. This angered Cromwell and he marched his New Model Army north to fight the Covenanters.

In 1650, the Scottish Covenanters suffered a terrible defeat at Dunbar despite a strong start. Illness spread through the Scottish camp and Cromwell showed no pity, killing up to 5,000 men and forcing a remaining 10,000 prisoners to march between 30 and 40 miles to Edinburgh. Those who did not die of starvation or disease were held captive and later sold as slaves, or forced to fight for Cromwell against the French and the Irish Catholics.

BATTLE OF DUNBAR
Where the Scots suffered a costly defeat.

OLIVER CROMWELL
Became a
tyrannical
dictator.

The Battle of Worcester took place in
1651 when the exiled Charles II mounted
a surprise attack while Cromwell was
campaigning in Scotland. Cromwell's
forces were much stronger and chased
the Royalist army to Worcester, where the
remaining Scottish Royalist Army was
defeated once and for all.

Cromwell also attacked Ireland, where
his ruthless killing of thousands of Catholics
is often regarded as near-genocidal. And
although many Scots died during his campaigns,
he is not as reviled in Scotland as he is in Ireland.

Cromwell's protectorate was almost a
dictatorship. He dissolved Parliament and set
up his own 'bare-bones' parliament. He began
to take on more and more of the trappings of
monarchy, even holding an event that mimicked
a coronation and which involved his being seated
on King Edward's Coronation Chair, like all other
'monarchs' before him.

When Cromwell died in 1658, his son, Richard, succeeded him as Lord Protector; however, he was a weak leader and had no real authority. This provided an opportunity for George Monck, leader of the New Model Army, to march back to London and restore Parliament. Soon afterwards, in 1660, Charles II was invited back from exile and the monarchy was restored.

Charles II was a popular king and restored many traditions that had been banned during Cromwell's puritan reign. The Great Plague swept through England and the Great Fire of London in 1666 paved the way for a remodelling of London and the building of many iconic landmarks, including the new St Paul's Cathedral.

CHARLES II
A popular king who reopened the theatres closed by Cromwell.

The Killing Times

After Charles II became King of England and Scotland in 1660, he rejected the Covenanters and reintroduced the Episcopalian way in Scotland.

Soon, rebel ministers began to preach in the open air. Charles II enacted oppressive laws against Covenant and Presbyterian practices, doling out harsh punishments for those found guilty. The oppressive regime led to several rebellions and battles between the poorly armed Covenanters and the king's men, most notably the Battle of Rullion Green (the Battle of Pentland Hills).

FIELD PREACHING
Rebels preached in the open air so as not to be discovered.

By 1679 the rebellion had gathered pace and the Covenanters won a surprise victory at the Battle of Drumclog, armed only with pitchforks and other tools.

The government saw the Covenanters as a minor problem that threatened social order and didn't put a great deal of energy or resources into dealing with the 'problem'.

By 1680 the Covenanters had taken it one step further and had prepared an underground document, known as the Sanquhar Declaration. Richard Cameron, who was an underground Covenanter and religious leader, wrote the declaration; his followers later became known as Cameronians. Although many Covenanters pretended to be loyal to the king, the Cameronians outwardly denounced Charles II and his Catholic brother, James.

MARTYRS

During the 'Killing Times', many Covenanters died for their cause and were remembered as martyrs. Their violent deaths are remembered on gravestones and memorials throughout Scotland. Despite their failure to restore a Covenanted Scotland, Covenanters are remembered as having been successful for the continuation of their religious practices both in Scotland and also in Ireland and North America (where many escaped persecution) and for not allowing the king to dictate his subjects' religion.

Field preacher's bible

COVENANTER FLAG
Was used during battles in the 17th century

This open rebellion marked a turning point and the period known as the 'Killing Times' began. The government set an example of the extremists by allowing indiscriminate public executions of suspected Covenanters without trial. Cameron was killed early on in the struggle, but his followers continued their fight. The issue came to a head in 1685 when James VII and II succeeded Charles. The refusal of the small band of militant Cameronians to acknowledge the King's authority led to the condemnation of the Cameronians by nearly all of the moderate Presbyterian ministry.

Over time (and after the defeat of a rebellion in 1685), there was rapprochement between many of the moderates and James VII. In 1687, James offered them toleration as long as they acknowledged his absolute authority. They were not natural bedfellows and James's policy of toleration alienated his Episcopalian allies. But there was another, Protestant, contender to the throne, William of Orange of the Netherlands, whose claim came through his wife Mary, James's daughter. Parliament wished for the country to remain Protestant and preferred William of Orange because his religious views were more appealing.

The struggle for the throne led to the Jacobite Risings (Jacobites were supporters of James VII). The Cameronians helped defeat the Jacobites during the revolution of 1689, cementing William's claim.

The Church of Scotland became Presbyterian once again. Most Covenanters accepted the settlement, but some Cameronians refused to acknowledge the authority of the Presbyterian Church.

COVENANTER MONUMENT
In Edinburgh for the dead of the Pentland Rising of 1666.

The Glorious Revolution

When King James VII and II was overthrown by Parliament, his daughter Mary, and her husband, William of Orange, took the throne.

James VII and II ruled Britain from 1685 to 1689, but his increasing religious tolerance and ties with both France and the Catholic religion were of great concern to Parliament. His daughter, Mary, who had married the Dutch Stadtholder, William of Orange, had been heir apparent to the English throne until the birth of her brother, James, in 1688. This changed the line of succession and meant that a Catholic succession seemed likely.

Parliament wanted the country to remain Protestant, fearing that an Anglo-French alliance would leave Britain in a weak position defensively. They turned to Mary and William of Orange. Motivated by the threat of an Anglo-French alliance, William agreed to invade Britain. The 'Glorious Revolution' soon succeeded in England, because of lack of support for

WILLIAM OF ORANGE
Conquered England at parliament's request.

the king; those who continued to support the exiled King James became known as Jacobites.

William's invasion of England had far-reaching effects in the American colonies and in Ireland and for the early 'Jacobite Rising of Dundee'. Soon oppressive laws against Catholics were introduced, with Catholics losing the right to vote, to sit in Parliament and to fight in an army. William was also responsible for the Act of Settlement in 1701, which prevented the accession of a Catholic to the throne, and prohibited the marriage of a monarch with a Catholic – a rule that still applies today. This ensured that Protestantism would be the dominant

JAMES VII OF SCOTLAND & II OF ENGLAND
An unpopular king.

DUTCH FLEET
Faced almost no opposition from English forces.

JACOBITE FLAG
Jacobite supporters
would wear a
white cloth in the
shape of a rose
on their clothes.

force in England and, despite an early uprising, the Jacobites retreated into exile until the union of 1707.

Before he died, William had wanted union – to secure his political settlement and deny the Jacobites a way back in Scotland. Under his successor, Queen Anne, the English and Scottish governments discussed union.

The English wanted to ensure that Scotland would not choose a monarch other than the reigning English monarch. Before his death, this had been of great concern to William, who was worried that separate monarchs might leave England open to attack from the French. At the time, Scotland was suffering at the hands of failed financial schemes and famine.

In fact a time was coming when the Scots would choose a monarch different from that of England (one descended from the Catholic James VII) whereas the English would choose a descendant from the House of Hanover (a Protestant line of succession). A few years later, costly and ill-fated expeditions meant that the Scottish economy was in difficulty, and it was felt that English assistance could save them. Furthermore, a large number of the better-off in Scotland got paid a sum of money if Scottish MPs agreed to union.

The Scottish economic problem came to a head in 1705 when England passed the Alien Act, which declared Scottish subjects 'aliens' in England unless Scotland would negotiate a union with England. The Treaty of Union was passed in 1707; it joined the two kingdoms of England and Scotland as one and Scotland became part of the United Kingdom of Great Britain.

The union was unpopular with most ordinary Scots, many Scottish MPs became notorious for corruption and vote buying and several unpopular taxes were brought in. However, the union opened up new markets that would eventually yield benefits.

BATTLE OF THE BOYNE
A turning point during 'The War of the Two Kings'.

The Massacre of Glencoe

A dark time in Scottish history when many members of the MacDonald clan of Glencoe were killed in their sleep by soldiers posing as friendly guests.

The Highland clans had taken part in the first Jacobite rising of 1689 following King William's accession to the throne. By 1691, William was willing to offer the clans a pardon for their part in the rebellion, but only if they agreed to pledge allegiance to him before 1 January 1692.

Many clans were slow to come forward, as they were waiting to see if the exiled King James would return, believing King William did not represent their interests. It was the Chief of the MacDonald clan of Glencoe, Alistair MacIain, who left it the latest – waiting until

GLENCOE PASS
Where many of the clan members fled.

31 December 1691 to make the journey to Fort William to take the oath. However, upon his arrival he was told he would have to travel to the Sheriff of Inveraray, 70 miles away, to take the oath. It took until 6 January for MacIain to take the oath, but despite this delay, he was assured that it had been accepted and that the MacDonald clan of Glencoe would be safe.

JOHN DALRYMPLE
Convinced King William to sign an order to expatriate the MacDonalds.

Many historians believe that John Dalrymple, who was Master of Stair and the Secretary of State, had been hoping that some Highlanders wouldn't take the oath and that he would be able to assert his authority. Word reached Dalrymple that MacDonald had not signed the oath by the date set by William and he sent 120 soldiers, led by Captain Robert Campbell, to Glencoe.

The soldiers posed as friendly officials, probably giving the impression that they were there to collect taxes. The Highlanders showed the soldiers hospitality, offering the troops food, drink and shelter for 10 days and nights.

**ROBERT CAMPBELL
OF GLENLYON**

Led his soldiers into
the brutal massacre.

This all came to an end on 12 February, when Campbell received orders to 'fall upon the rebels […] and to ensure no man escapes'. The massacre began early the next morning when MacIain was killed in his bed. Many houses were set alight and men were bound and gagged before they were killed. The gunfire woke other members of the clan, who fled into the mountains. Thirty-eight men, women and children were killed at Glencoe, with many more dying of exposure and exhaustion, having tried to escape across mountainous regions during the winter months.

The massacre was described under Scots law as a 'murder under trust', which was a far worse crime than ordinary murder. Despite the horrific events and the act of mass murder by the state against its own people, no one was ever brought to trial. The massacre of the MacDonald clan served as a warning to other clans and, although Dalrymple masterminded the event, King William could not deny that he had signed the orders for their deaths.

The Massacre of Glencoe backfired on Dalrymple, re-igniting a dwindling passion in the exiled Jacobites, which would come to a head in the Jacobite Rising of 1745.

FLEEING CLAN MEMBERS
Were chased and killed or left to die of exposure in the cold mountains of the Highlands.

Scotland's Empire

Much like the English, Portuguese and Spanish, Scottish pioneers journeyed to foreign lands and attempted to build colonies of their own.

DARIEN CHEST
Used to store money made by the Company of Scotland during their failed conquest of Darien (now Panama).

The first Scottish colony was founded between 1629 and 1632 when Sir William Alexander, a Scottish explorer, claimed part of what is now Canada for Scotland. He named the land Nova Scotia, meaning New Scotland. Unfortunately, the area was already a French colony and fighting soon broke out. Only a few years after Scotland's first colony had been established, Charles I sold Nova Scotia back to the French.

Scotland had made several attempts during the late 1600s to expand its overseas trade. However, the English parliament had introduced a law restricting imported goods, which meant that only goods carried on English ships could be traded. Added to this, the English had monopolised trade in India and Africa and Scottish traders were finding their options becoming more and more limited. However, Scottish merchants soon realised that they could exploit the ambiguities of sharing a king but not a tax system with England by conducting trade with willing colonials.

In 1695, William Paterson, co-founder of the Bank of England, helped to create the Company of Scotland Trading to Africa and the Indies. The company had a 31-year monopoly over new trade with Africa and Asia and was permitted to colonise any uninhabited areas of America, Asia or Africa. Paterson's risky plan to revive Scotland's economic position against England was based around the area known as Darien, the narrow bit of land that separates North and South America in modern-day Panama. Paterson chose this area of land as he believed it would facilitate a good

DARIEN

The Scots were unprepared for the tropical conditions and unfamiliar illnesses of this foreign land.

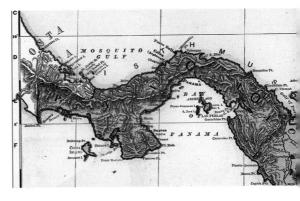

**SCOTTISH
SETTLEMENTS**

Plans for the Scottish
colony of New
Caledonia in Darien
were drawn up
before the settlers
reached the land.

trading route between Europe and the
East Indies that avoided the treacherous
journey around the Cape of Good Hope
in southern Africa.

Under pressure from King William,
all English merchants had to pull out of
Paterson's funding deal and the £400,000
capital required to fund the project now
came directly from Scotland's economy.
The Scots set sail with bibles, fancy
clothing, shoes and pipes – showing
little or no knowledge of the climate
in Darien, or New Caledonia, as it was
going to be named. The Scots were unaware that the
land they were travelling to had a hot and humid
climate where malaria was rife and, more importantly,
that the land already belonged to the King of Spain.
Before the first settlers could report back, the Scots
sent two further groups of settlers out to Darien.

By 1699 inadequate supplies, disease and
exhaustion had killed over a quarter of the settlers.

The new colony sought assistance from the nearby English colony of Jamaica and, although help had been promised, it transpired that King William had forbidden colonial officials to provide aid – this was because he was trying to forge an alliance with Spain and didn't want to offend them; the Spanish attacked the Scottish who had settled in their land, wiping out almost all of those who remained alive.

The Darien scheme became known as one of Scotland's worst colonial disasters and added to Scotland's financial woes. Many wealthy Scots were out of pocket and that swayed some of them towards a vote for union in 1707.

NOVA SCOTIA
Scotland's first, short-lived colony in modern-day Canada.

The '45 Jacobite Rising

The last Jacobite Rising, often called the 'Forty-Five', took place when King James's grandson, Prince Charles Edward, tried to regain the throne.

DUNCAN STEWART
A famous Highlander who supported Bonnie Prince Charlie and the Jacobite cause.

Jacobites were dedicated to the restoration of the lineage of the Stuart kings. The Jacobite movement was a response to the deposition of James VII and II and changing the royal lineage to the firmly Protestant House of Hanover. Many Jacobites, particularly Irish Catholics who had been discriminated against by new Protestant legislation hoped that a returning Stuart dynasty would end the repression known as the penal laws.

In 1744, Prince Charles Edward (Bonnie Prince Charlie) left Rome to help the French attack England. However, the French lost interest and Charles realised the only hope of inciting a Jacobite rebellion would be through his own actions. As the grandson of the exiled King James VII and II, he had a claim to the

British throne, which is why he is often referred to as 'The Young Pretender'.

Charles sailed from France to Scotland and started to muster an army that would overthrow the new King George II. He attracted over 1,000 followers – many of them Highland clan members.

In 1745, Britain was engaged in a European war, which meant they had only a reserve force with which to fight Charles. The British army was easily evaded and Charles's men went on to take back several Scottish towns, including Perth, Coatbridge and Edinburgh, declaring James VII's son, James VIII, king. At this point, Charles appealed to the French for weapons,

HOLYROOD PALACE
Charles held court here for five weeks.

BATTLE OF CULLODEN
Where Charles was
overpowered by
the British.

for support and for them to invade England. While
Charles's army grew stronger and headed south, the
English rallied their overseas troops. Many began to
doubt French support that had been promised and
although Charles had made it as far south as Derby,
rumours of a strong defensive army in London meant
his followers retreated north to await the French.
However, the French got wind of the retreat and
aborted their invasion.

Despite strong support from many Highlanders,
Charles didn't have the backing of all
Scots, many of whom supported
the Protestant succession and
had come to believe that the
Stuarts were tyrants and
now felt the economic
benefit of free trade
through union. Charles
continued on his quest
– by now his army

had grown to over 8,000 men. Charles won a further victory at Falkirk, but his army kept missing the French attempts to resupply them. At the Battle of Culloden, near Inverness, the so far successful tactic of the Highland charge finally failed due to confused orders and a disciplined British army.

Charles fled from the battle, blaming his commanders and disloyal troops for the defeat. His escape through the Highlands and to France became legendary; he even disguised himself as a lady's maid to flee from the Isle of Skye.

This was the closest the Jacobites had come to toppling the House of Hanover. Poor leadership and a superior British army meant the Jacobites were finally defeated. The '45 Rising also sparked a new government policy that would protect Britain from any further rebellion – the Highlands were garrisoned and mapped and large forts were constructed. Clan chiefs were stripped of their powers, Highland culture was repressed and tartan was outlawed.

FLORA MACDONALD
Helped Bonnie Prince Charlie escape back to France.

Bonnie Prince Charlie

Best remembered as the leader of the failed '45 Jacobite Rising. Charles's escape from Scotland has made him a heroic figure in Scottish folklore.

BONNIE PRINCE CHARLIE
A youthful portrait from the prince's time in Rome.

Charles Edward Stuart was born in Rome in 1720; he was the grandson of the exiled King James VII and II and believed that he had a claim to the British throne. He grew up in Rome and lived a privileged life as part of the Stuart dynasty. Like his father, he was a Catholic and a strong supporter of the Jacobite cause to reinstate the Stuart monarchy in Britain.

From a young age, Charles received military training and, in 1744, he travelled to France with the intention of becoming a commander of the French army and instigating an invasion of England from there. His plans nearly succeeded, but the French naval fleet became disoriented by a storm, which gave the British the time they needed to form a defensive line in the Channel.

Undeterred by this initial failure, Charles continued on his mission to restore the Stuart dynasty and spearheaded his own campaign against the British. He sailed to Scotland alone and mustered an army made up of Highland clans and Irish Catholics.

Charles led the rebellion with stubbornness. He refused to listen to advice from his best commander, Lord George Murray, and this eventually led to his downfall at the Battle of Culloden.

Charles fled the battle with a £30,000 bounty on his head. For a year he wandered the Highlands of Scotland drinking heavily, blaming others for his defeat and conducting several affairs. He eventually escaped from the Isle of Skye by dressing up as Lady Flora MacDonald's Irish maid, Betty Burke.

BONNIE PRINCE CHARLIE MONUMENT
This monument, with Loch Seaforth in the background, commemorates the landing of Bonnie Prince Charlie after his defeat and escape from Culloden in May 1746.

THE SKYE BOAT SONG

The Skye Boat Song is a Scottish folk song that recounts the escape of Bonnie Prince Charlie to the Isle of Skye after his defeat at the Battle of Culloden. Although it was written well after the event, the song expresses strong Jacobite views and helped to secure Charles as a Scottish legend.

Speed, bonnie boat, like a bird on the wing,
Onward! The sailors cry;
Carry the lad that's born to be King,
Over the sea to Skye.

CHARLES' STATUE
In Derby, from where his army retreated back to Scotland.

Charles spent the remainder of his life in exile in France and Italy. This period of his life was considerably less romantic than the songs and stories of his courage in Scotland make out. He grew old and bitter, drinking heavily and was even prepared to renounce his faith to give him a better chance at reclaiming the crown. Charles' marriage to Princess Louise of Stolberg-Gedern in 1772 was marred by rumours of adultery and abuse. After only eight years of marriage, Louise left him for another man. Charles died in Rome in 1788 and was buried by his brother, Cardinal Henry Benedict Stuart.

Although the true story of Bonnie Prince Charlie is much less glamorous than that of the romantic stories, poems and songs of Scottish folklore, Charles is still remembered in Scotland with affection as the man who nearly toppled the House of Hanover.

ISLE OF SKYE
From where Charles escaped, dressed as Betty Burke.

ST PETER'S BASILICA
In Rome, where Charles' remains were transferred in 1807.

The Battle of Culloden

Taking place on 16 April 1746, this was the last battle fought on British soil and saw the end of the Jacobite campaign to restore the Stuart dynasty.

CULLODEN MOORE
Battlefield and memorial.

The battle ended the doomed Jacobite Rising of 1745, which was led by a misguided Charles Edward Stuart (Bonnie Prince Charlie). Charles, the grandson of the exiled James VII and II, had returned to Scotland to attempt to overthrow the ruling house of Hanover and restore the Stuart dynasty to the British throne. Charles' followers, the Jacobites, were typically Highlanders, Scottish Episcopalians and Irish Catholics who were being oppressed by the penal laws brought in to protect Protestant rule in Britain.

Charles' campaign started well – because the British were fighting in Europe, the small army left behind was inexperienced and was almost toppled by Charles' men. However, the British army returned to defend King George II and an army led by his son, the Duke of Cumberland, met Charles's army at the agreed site of Drumossie Moor, near Inverness.

THE JACOBITE ARMY

A large percentage of the Jacobite army was made up of Highland clansmen who were either Catholic, or Episcopalians who practised a different form of the Protestant faith from that enforced by the king. Many Highlanders, however, were forced to join the cause by clan chiefs or their landlords, and desertion became a big problem for Charles. Charles' men also lacked training, weapons and armour. By the time of the battle his army was tired, disorganised and ill-prepared to fight.

The Battle of Culloden

HANOVERIAN SOLDIER
Who fought for the
British army.

The night before the battle, Charles' right-hand man, Lord George Murray, suggested a surprise attack on the government troops, probably knowing this was their only chance of winning. However, setting off in the dark led to confusion and miscommunication. Murray decided to save energy and turn back, but his message to retreat did not reach the other half of the army, who carried on. When the Jacobites made contact with the government army, they realised that half their number had already returned home and they, too, turned back. By the time the Jacobites returned to base they were tired and had dispersed to find food and shelter. It was not long until news came that the government soldiers were advancing.

The site of the battle, the moorland around Culloden and Drumossie, turned out to be a bad choice, and although Murray had advised Charles against the location, the battle went ahead. The ground was rough and marshy and weather conditions would most likely have blown the wind and rain into the faces of the Jacobite army. With a force armed only with swords and daggers, Charles' Highland charge tactic was no match for the guns and cannons of the government army. It is possible that this monumental defeat happened because Charles was overly confident going into battle, following early victories against an inexperienced reserve army, who had only had to fight until the highly trained soldiers returned to fight on the government side.

The battle did not last long. The Jacobite army suffered heavy losses, with only a minor loss of life suffered by the government troops. Charles deserted his army, fled to the Highlands and eventually escaped to France, never to return.

Although many Jacobite soldiers were Scottish, it is worth noting that this was not a war between the Scottish and the English; in fact, many Scots supported the British government.

HIGHLAND SOLDIER
Who fought for Bonnie Prince Charlie.

The Enlightenment

Also known as the 'Golden Age', the Enlightenment was an intellectual movement that swept across Europe during the 18th century.

JAMES WATT
One of Scotland's most famous inventors and engineers.

By the mid-1700s, many Scots were literate and well educated. Several clubs had sprung up within Scotland's universities, including the Select Society at the University of Edinburgh. Since the Renaissance, people had begun to view the world from a more humanist angle, looking to science and logic, rather than religion, for the explanation of many of the Earth's mysteries. Like many in Europe, Scotland's thinkers began to place huge importance on reason and man's ability to rationalise; they believed positive changes in society could be achieved only through reason and a philosophy that considered not only individual benefit, but the benefit of society as a whole. This notion became known as utilitarianism; today, it is the basis of nearly all modern social orders around the world.

Scotland's Enlightenment did not stop with philosophy; the 18th century saw advances in several important scientific fields, such as engineering, architecture, medicine, geology and chemistry, which would change the world forever.

Scotland had its fair share of influential thinkers during the Europe-wide Enlightenment, the first major philosopher being Francis Hutcheson. Hutcheson led the philosophy programme at Glasgow University and developed many utilitarian and consequentialist theories, which he believed, with Jeremy Bentham, would provide 'the greatest happiness for the greatest number'.

At the same time, people began to question religious understanding of the Earth's mysteries. Instead of believing in the old superstitions, Scottish thinkers, such as David Hume, held the new scientific ideas of Copernicus, Galileo and Newton in high esteem. This shift in thinking led to great leaps forward in Scottish understanding of science, medicine and the mysteries of the Earth.

FRANCIS HUTCHESON
One of the founding fathers of the Scottish Enlightenment.

STEAM LOCOMOTIVE
The icon of the industrial revolution.

Many Scottish thinkers from this time were dissatisfied with the old theological disputes and looked to science and reason to bring about scientific progress. Some of the key figures at this time were James Anderson, who pioneered discoveries linking plants to food and fuel; Joseph Black, who became the first person to discover latent heat and how to isolate carbon dioxide; William Cullen, who

ADAM SMITH

A philosopher best remembered for his economic masterpiece, *The Wealth of Nations*, which is regarded as the first modern work of economics and one of the most influential books ever published. Many believe Smith's ideas were the catalyst and main influence behind what eventually became the free market. He also had an influence on our modern tax system, stating:

'The subject of every state ought to contribute towards the support of the government in proportion to their respective abilities.'

Adam Smith's portrait is featured on the English £20 bank note and the Scottish £50 note.

JAMES MADISON
The fourth President of the USA was directly influenced by the Scottish Enlightenment.

became a figurehead for the development of medicine throughout the world; and James Hutton, the first modern geologist.

The Scottish Enlightenment had a far-reaching effect, not only in scientific and philosophical matters, but also in the realms of art and music. Scotland became one of the top places in the world to study, with Edinburgh training facilities, such as the College of Surgeons and the University of Edinburgh, becoming beacons in the medical profession. Scottish philosophy and political ideas spread throughout the British Empire. Earlier Scottish emigration to America meant that the ideas of the Enlightenment went on to influence the Founding Fathers of the USA following its split from the British Empire; Scottish philosophy on common sense, reason and realism also influenced American thinkers throughout the 19th century.

David Hume

Often regarded as Scotland's greatest philosopher, Hume was a rationalist and empiricist and became a key figure of the Scottish Enlightenment.

FAMOUS STATUE
Outside St Giles'
Cathedral, Edinburgh.

Along with many other thinkers of the time, including John Locke and George Berkeley, Hume was an empiricist, which meant he believed that human knowledge comes only from our own first-hand experience. He believed that rationalism, together with experience and evidence, gave rise to the formation of ideas. This was a theory that clashed directly with the church, which expected people to believe without question and to continue traditions passed down through generations. Empiricism is the basis of all modern scientific experiments and calls for all ideas and theories to be tested via observation, rather than relying on intuition or mystical revelation.

WAS HUME AN ATHEIST?

Hume is often regarded as the first atheist; however, he never publicly stated his disbelief in God, most likely for reasons of self-preservation. However, Hume had a problem with an unquestioning belief in God, arguing that proof was surely required in order to establish a truth. The French philosopher, Voltaire, along with many of his contemporaries, shared Hume's beliefs. However, it is possible that Hume was agnostic rather than atheist since he could neither prove, nor disprove, the existence of God.

DAVID HUME
Scotland's greatest philosopher.

Hume is best known for his work *A Treatise of Human Nature*, which explored the motivations of man and the psychological rationale behind human nature. Unlike many around him at the time and famous predecessors, including Descartes, Hume believed that man was driven not by reason, but by desire.

Hume went on to anger the religious authorities further with his discussions on miracles. Since he could not prove the existence of God, Hume believed the only proof available to us was miracles. Miracles went diectly against Hume's

RELIGIOUS HEALING
Hume argued
against miracles
as historic fact.

theory of empiricism, which held that people should only believe that something had happened based on their experience of life. A miracle goes directly against what we reason to be possible; therefore when we read or hear the report of a miraculous event (such as Jesus walking on water, or a statue of the Virgin Mary crying), this contradicts our belief that such things could normally happen. While Hume did not entirely deny the possibility that miracles may have occurred, since he wasn't there to experience first-hand whether or not they happened, he made several rational arguments against miracles based on his experience of human nature:

• People lie, either to benefit their religion or to benefit their social standing.

• People revel in passing on stories of improbable events because they are exciting; examples of folklore show how these stories have become exaggerated.

• Miracles always happen in places where people are uneducated and less civilised, perhaps because a more civilised society would see through the illusion or not be impressed at all.

• Miracles from different religions contradict miracles from other religions; therefore, even if some were true, they would still contradict each other.

Hume was a great sceptic and often insulted those of blind faith by calling them gullible and ignorant. Although he ruffled many feathers during his lifetime, his work and ideas have lived on and influenced many others, including Kant and Einstein. His scepticism and belief in logic and experience laid the groundwork for new ways of thinking and approaching all aspects of science, economics, philosophy and sociology that we still hold true today.

BUDDHISM

Hume learnt a lot about Buddhist thought during his time in France.

Glasgow and the Americans

The port of Glasgow was ideally placed to exploit new trade opportunities; by the 1770s, Glasgow had a monopoly on the British tobacco market.

Before the Union of 1707, Scottish merchants had already penetrated American and Caribbean colonies, often by evading English trade laws. However, post 1707 Scots could exploit new legal trading opportunities across the Atlantic on a larger scale.

SHIPPING
Glasgow became rich from trade with the USA.

The Scots failed to break into the slave trade from Africa, but did exploit slaves through their successful penetration of the plantation system in America and the Caribbean, repatriating the

profits generated. The main commodities to come from this area were tobacco, sugar and cotton.

During the early to mid-1700s the tobacco trade went through the British port of Bristol, but in 1674, the first shipment reached the port of Glasgow. Its superior location meant that only a few years later Glasgow was dominating the tobacco market in Britain. Glasgow merchants suddenly became very rich and powerful and were known as tobacco lords. Even today, their success can be seen in their elegant houses and street names such as Virginia and Jamaica Streets. The area known as Merchant City developed, with warehouses and impressive residences being built.

THE MERCHANT CITY TRAIL
In Glasgow takes you on a historical tour of Glasgow's trading heritage.

Glasgow merchants soon became involved with the sugar, tea and cotton trades too, and Glasgow's industry and prestige boomed. The Tobacco Lords and other merchants of Glasgow made their money re-exporting goods throughout the rest of Europe.

At this time a great deal of money was invested in industry and housing, and soon the city spread further west. The heavy investment in factories and equipment laid the foundations for the industrial revolution.

In 1775, the American War of Independence saw America split from Britain. A system of stockpiling tobacco on credit meant that American plantations were heavily in debt to Glasgow merchants. Once free from Britain, America was free to trade directly with the rest of Europe and this meant that the tobacco merchants in Britain became redundant.

Glasgow merchants switched their trade from tobacco to cotton, which came from the British-owned West Indies and still required the use of British ports.

GLASGOW PORT TODAY
Is still important to trade in Britain.

Between 1750 and 1821, Glasgow's population

experienced a huge expansion, from around 30,000 to nearly 150,000 inhabitants. It became a popular destination for emigrating Irish Protestants, who shared their ancestry and culture with the Lowland Scots. Many of the new immigrants were skilled in handloom weaving; with help from the cotton trade Glasgow became an independent cotton-weaving community.

Glasgow's development into an industrial city depended on a revolutionary scheme to deepen the River Clyde, which allowed ocean-going vessels to venture further inland. This brought an increase in trade since merchants no longer had to rely on Glasgow's outports. The expansion in trade also meant that Glasgow's merchants and manufacturers became influential in government.

TEMPLETON FACTORY
One of Glasgow's most famous factories has now been converted into apartments.

Robert Burns

Born in 1759, Robert Burns is Scotland's most famous writer and is widely regarded as the national poet of Scotland.

He is best known for his poems, written either in the Scots language, or in English in a Scottish idiom, which made his poetry accessible to a wider audience. Burns was a key figure of the Romantic movement, which swept through Scotland towards the end of the 18th century, during the Scottish Enlightenment.

During his early career, Burns was known for his casual love affairs; in 1785 he fathered his first child by his mother's servant, while at the same time conducting a relationship with Jean Armour, who also became pregnant a year later. Burns later married Armour, much to his father's disapproval. By 1786 Burns had fallen in love with another woman, Mary Campbell, with whom he planned to emigrate to Jamaica; he was offered a job as a bookkeeper on a

ROBERT BURNS
Regarded as the national poet of Scotland.

plantation and was planning to go, despite his liberal views and later poems that condemned slavery. However, he didn't have the money to pay for his journey to the West Indies, which is when a friend, Gavin Hamilton, suggested he publish his poems, and this was the beginning of a successful literary career.

Burns was born into poverty, but benefited from educational reforms at that time, which made him a true success story of the Scottish Enlightenment. Burns first published his work in Kilmarnock; *Poems Chiefly in the Scottish Dialect* (1786) sold out within a few weeks and this initial triumph encouraged him to take his writing to Edinburgh, where he kept company with the leaders of literary society. His Edinburgh edition of the same work earned him enough money to tour other areas of Scotland, including the Borders and Highlands, where his work was also greatly admired.

Because of Burns' humble background, his work was accessible to all and dealt with subjects to which everyone could relate. This is a key factor in his success

BURNS STATUE IN DUMFRIES
One of many throughout Scotland.

and, although much of his work was written in the Scots language, he has been translated more widely than any other Scottish writer.

As well as poems, Burns loved to collect and rewrite folk songs he had heard during his tours of Scotland. Some of his most famous works even have ceremonial use today, such as *Auld Lang Syne*, which is sung to celebrate the New Year, not just in Scotland, but around the English-speaking world, and *Scots Wha Hae*, often sung as the unofficial Scottish national anthem.

BURNS' HOUSE
The birthplace of Robert Burns in Alloway, Scotland.

BURNS NIGHT

Burns Night is often regarded as the second national day of Scotland, behind St Andrew's Day. It is celebrated on 25 January, which was Burns' birthday. Traditional Burns suppers feature a haggis, and Burns' famous *Address to a Haggis* is read out before it is stabbed dramatically. A Scotch whisky toast is then proposed and only after this can people begin eating. After the meal various speeches are given remembering Burns' life or poetry. There is often a 'Toast to the Lassies', given by a male guest, which is followed by a 'Reply to the Toast to the Lassies', which is given by a female guest. The evening is usually ended with a rendition of *Auld Lang Syne*.

Burns is best remembered for his romantic poems, such as *Ae Fond Kiss*, and humorous poems, such as *Tam O'Shanter*. However, many of his poems had a political edge and were influenced by the French Revolution, with which he sympathised. His radical views alienated him from friends and he became despondent and fell into ill health. He died aged just 37, yet through his 12 children, he now has over 600 living descendants.

HAGGIS
Famously eaten on Burns night, when Burns' famous 'Address to a Haggis' is read.

James Hutton

James Hutton is often regarded as the father of geology and his work forms the basis of nearly all modern geological theory.

JAMES HUTTON
The father of
modern geology.

Hutton was born in 1726. His father, an Edinburgh merchant, died when he was only three; his mother insisted on a good education for her children, and by the age of 14 Hutton was able to attend the University of Edinburgh, first as a student of humanities and, later, chemistry. Although a qualified doctor, Hutton never practised medicine and instead became a farmer in England and later in Berwickshire. During his time farming he developed a keen interest in geology.

Hutton returned to Edinburgh in 1767, where he bought a house that overlooked the Salisbury Crags. The unusual rock formations intrigued Hutton and his passion for geology truly came to life.

Hutton had an influential role in the Scottish Enlightenment, which saw many great minds come together and forge advances in philosophy, science and

economics, thrusting Scotland into a new age.

Hutton was greatly involved in the Forth and Clyde Canal, which deepened the riverbed of the Clyde. The consequent increase in trade into Glasgow made the city one of Europe's biggest trading destinations.

However, Hutton is best remembered for his theory on rock formations. His *Theory of the Earth* (published in 1785) took 25 years to complete and is considered a cornerstone of the modern rationalist view of the world. He concluded that rock cycles shaped the earth we walk on over thousands of years, with old rocks being destroyed and broken down by weather, and new ones being formed by sediment.

OLD ROCKS
Examining rock formations helped Hutton establish his theory of deep time.

MADDER PLANT
Hutton developed a red dye from the roots of the madder plant.

Hutton's ideas were the basis of evolutionary theory. While many religious leaders who believed the earth was only 6,000 years old shunned them, his theories had a huge impact on 19th-century thinking.

Having observed hot springs and volcanoes, Hutton was one of the first to propose that the core of the earth was hot, and he believed it was this heat that caused the creation of new rock. He also concluded that land would be eroded by water and air over time and its sediment would be heated to create new rock. This revelation gave birth to a new concept, deep time.

FORTH AND CLYDE
Hutton helped build the Forth and Clyde Canal.

Through his study of rock formations, Hutton concluded that the Earth must be much older than originally believed from teachings in the Bible. His argument was based on the fact that the changes in rock that he had noted could not

have happened over a short period of time and, since these processes were still happening, he concluded that the Earth must be millions of years old.

Hutton also studied rain and produced his own theory of rain, which concluded that rainfall is directly related to the humidity of the air and the mixing of air currents in the atmosphere.

Hutton's ideas and unique approach to studying the Earth established geology as a proper science. The 'Great Age of Earth' was the first revolutionary concept to emerge from this school of thought. Although Hutton believed that species were designed to adapt to their situation, he believed this design came from God. His ideas, however, inspired dramatic thinkers, such as Darwin, who built on the deep time principle and on how land formations evolved to show how species also evolved over millions of years. Hutton's work inspired prolific scientists, such as Charles Lyell, author of the influential work, *Principles of Geology*.

SALISBURY CRAGS
Its interesting rock formation was so attractive to Hutton that he built his own house here.

The Radicals

The Radical War of 1820 was prompted by an economic downturn that highlighted the outdated practices of the ruling government.

REVOLUTIONS
Such as those in France and America, inspired the Scottish radicals.

In the 18th century, weavers and craftsmen were able to work for commission, which meant they could set their own hours and enjoy a positive work-life balance. However, by the beginning of the 19th century, the average wage of a weaver had halved. The devaluation of the work of weavers continued, forcing many into poverty. This sparked general strikes and demands for reform.

At this time, Scottish people were more educated than their neighbours in England. The Church promoted literacy and Scots were allowed to read in their own language. Robert Burns, whose widely available work had strong political messages, struck a chord with many ordinary workers. Thomas Paine's famous *Rights of Man* (1791) was read by many and popularised ideas of universal suffrage and republicanism.

The French and American Revolutions of the late 18th century revealed corruption and flaws in British society and the ruling classes, and many believed that, as in France, the ancient system of privilege could be toppled. Ordinary people could now group together and put themselves in a position of power. The social mobility of Scottish craftsmen, middle classes, merchants and philosophers made possible by the Enlightenment meant that societies could form and reformist ideas could be discussed.

The Peterloo Massacre of 1819 saw a cavalry charge on protesters who had gathered in Manchester to demand political reform. But rather than quash rebellion, this sparked further demonstrations throughout Britain.

HANDLOOM WEAVERS
As well as other artisans, had their wages halved.

The British gentry feared a revolution like that in America or France and recruited spies, informers and double agents to infiltrate the radicals.

Committees of radicals formed and met in taverns. Amongst them was John King, a spy who caused many ringleaders and radicals to be arrested. Plans to establish a provisional government and to separate England from Scotland were revealed – the British were tipped off and prepared themselves for battle.

The proclamation for a provisional government

STRIKES
Took place throughout Scotland.

was signed on 1 April 1820 and a series of strikes followed. Two radicals, Andrew Hardie and John Baird, were prepared to march on Carron, but they were betrayed by King and arrested. Strikes and marches continued but were easily quashed by the British military.

Eighty-eight men were charged with treason, with many executed at Stirling Castle. The rebellion was crushed and the Scots were appeased by a visit to Scotland from King George IV. The event helped to promote a Scottish national identity, and many unemployed were given new work. Electoral reform followed and Scotland's interests were represented in the British parliament.

The radical martyrs were pardoned in 1835 and became examples of courage and heroism for those living in fear of oppressive regimes. They paved the way for reform and gave others the courage to challenge an increasingly powerful industrial state. Although the rising was over, it had sparked the beginning of the radical movement.

GLASGOW GREEN
Where 40,000 workers met to demand greater political representation.

The Highland Clearances

The Highland clearances had a devastating effect on Gaelic culture and clan society, driving people from land they had called home for centuries.

During the late 18th century and early 19th century, many Highland estates made the switch from arable farming, which supported a large tenant population, to more profitable sheep farming. Tenants were no longer needed to work the land and so they were literally 'cleared' off it.

Many of those living in the Highlands were given little to no warning and were often evicted with brutal force. 1792, which became known as the 'Year of the Sheep', saw a huge wave of mass emigration, and although some purpose-built towns were created for displaced Highlanders, there wasn't enough

CROFT HOUSES
Now abandoned, were the typical dwellings of Highlanders.

accommodation and many were put on ships to Nova Scotia, South Carolina and other American colonies. Others were simply left to fend for themselves, often being left on exposed coastlines with no shelter.

CLAN TARTAN
Was banned during the 18th and 19th centuries.

As had happened in Ireland, the potato crop failed and this, together with the outbreak of disease, caused the deaths of even more Highlanders. Although some were given financial incentives to leave the land, historical records show that most landlords used force to evict their tenants.

By 1822, the second phase of clearances began and these were much more brutal. The Highland population and culture had once and for all been wiped out. And although their customs and the clan system had been repressed since the failed Jacobite Risings, the widespread clearances marked the end of their way of life.

SCOTTISH COAST
Highlanders were forced to move to rugged coastal areas, where farming was impossible, and were expected to take up fishing.

Even today, there are more sheep than people in the Scottish Highlands. Since so many Highlanders emigrated there is now a stronger representation of Gaelic speakers and Highland culture in North America and Australia than there is in Scotland.

Although the British government maintained that the clearances, or 'improvements', as they called them, were simply a consequence of agricultural and industrial change, many believe it was an early form of ethnic cleansing and it remains an emotive issue to this day. Many of the Highlanders were Episcopalian and had supported the Jacobite Risings in both Scotland and Ireland. They were viewed as less civilised than the rest of the population, and their ancient, militaristic clan system would still have been seen as a threat to the British establishment. The ruling class in Scotland was easily swayed into evicting them from the land in order to preserve its own wealth and social status.

As justification, landlords claimed that the Highlanders were lazy and work-shy, so sheep farming was simply a logical solution. Bad harvests and poor weather also meant that landlords needed to find a new way of earning money from the land. In some cases, the decision to leave was voluntary, as Highlanders had heard of new opportunities in the thriving United States of America.

Ironically for the landlords, the promised wealth of sheep farming proved to be a flash in the pan. Instead of providing meat for the growing industrial cities and wool to the factories, sheep farming quickly proved unsustainable and the landlords were undercut by cheaper and better quality products from Australia and New Zealand – lands to which many Highlanders had been forced to emigrate.

HIGHLANDERS EMIGRATE
Today there are more people of Highland descent in Australia than in Scotland.

POTATO FAMINE
Scared landlords into forcing eviction on their Highland tenants.

Sir Walter Scott

Walter Scott is regarded as one of Scotland's greatest writers. He was most famous for his historical novels and romantic poetry.

Scott was born in 1771. He contracted polio at the age of two and spent much of his early life travelling around Scotland for treatment and possible cures for the lameness it had given him. He was taught to read by his aunt, Jenny, and when he was 12, he began studying classics at Edinburgh University.

Having lived in the Scottish countryside, he developed a fascination with the folklore and oral story-telling tradition of the Scottish Borders. His first works were retellings of stories he had heard and translations of German ballads. In 1796, his friend, James Ballantyne, founded a printing press, enabling Scott to publish his own work. His published poems received critical acclaim and in 1813 he was offered the position of Poet Laureate, which he declined.

WALTER SCOTT
One of Scotland's most celebrated writers.

Scott went on to write several novels, his most famous being *The Bride of Lammermoor*, *Ivanhoe* and the series of novels published as *Tales of my Landlord*. His novels romanticised historical events, often intertwining fiction with real life events.

GLASGOW MONUMENT
To Walter Scott is now a famous landmark.

RECOVERY OF THE CROWN JEWELS

Walter Scott is often remembered for recovering the Scottish Crown Jewels, or Honours of Scotland, as they were also known. Ever since the Treaty of Union in 1707, which saw the union of the English and Scottish parliaments, the Scottish crown, sword of state and sceptre were kept in Scotland. However, because they were seen as a symbol of Scottish independence, they had to be hidden away in a strongbox in the Crown Room of Edinburgh Castle. The room was secured with barred doors, the keys for which had been conveniently lost. Scott believed that the Honours could be unearthed and set up a commission to trace them. The doors were broken apart and the Honours of Scotland were found, untouched. They are the earliest surviving crown jewels in Europe and can been seen today on display in Edinburgh Castle's Crown Room.

In 1825, the Ballantyne printing business, in which Scott had invested heavily, went bankrupt following a banking crisis in Great Britain. Scott was ruined, but rather than accept help from his fans, he sold his assets and embarked on a grand tour of Europe, intending to produce a biography of Napoleon Bonaparte. But by 1831 his health was in decline and he returned to Scotland. He died in 1832 and, although he was in tremendous financial trouble, the popularity of his work eventually paid off his debts.

Scott is generally regarded as the father of the modern historical novel and his work appeals to children and adults alike. His work led to a greater understanding of Highland culture, which had been regarded as barbaric and dangerous.

EDINBURGH UNIVERSITY
Where Scott first studied at the age of 12.

His novels helped Scotland relegate even recent historical events to the past and cemented the belief that the country had entered a new, modern age of capitalism.

Scott is commemorated in several parts of Scotland – tributes include the Scott Monument on Princes Street in Edinburgh and the monument in George Square in Glasgow. There is even a statue of Scott in Central Park, Manhattan. Edinburgh's main railway station was named after his first novel, *Waverley*.

WALTER SCOTT MONUMENT
In Edinburgh is one of Scotland's grandest monuments.

FROM C. R. LESLIE, R.A.

RAVENSWOOD AND LUCY AT THE MERMAIDEN'S WELL.

As they arose to leave the fountain which had been the witness of their mutual engagement, an arrow whistled through the air, and struck a raven perched on the sere branch of an old oak.—PAGE 193.

BRIDE OF LAMMERMOOR
Inspired art by Charles Robert Leslie; this picture depicts the two main characters, Lucy Ashton and Edgar Ravenswood.

Clans and Tartan

Tartan in Scotland dates back to Roman times and possibly earlier, but the Clan tartans we know today are from the 19th century.

BONNIE SCOTLAND.

HIGHLAND MARCH.
By
JOHN PRIDHAM.

Tartan is made up of interlocking horizontal and vertical bands of wool woven in different colours. Although tartan is particularly associated with Scotland, it was known to be worn by Celts and other Europeans. It is now also popular in America, possibly due to Scottish emigration following the Highland clearances.

Tartan is always the material of Scottish kilts and this traditional dress was often worn by Highlanders. Until the late 1800s, tartan was associated with the various Highland regions rather than specific clans; this is because tartan garments would have been produced by local weavers who used their own patterns and colours depending on what natural dyes were available.

It was only from the mid-19th century onwards that specific tartans became associated with Scottish Clans or families, or indeed institutions that wanted to be associated with Scottish heritage. Although tartan, kilts and Scottish dress became synonymous with Highland culture, the notion that the various colours and patterns had specific meanings is a modern invention.

The most common tartan patterns are Black Watch and Royal Stuart. Black Watch was designed in 1725 by the Highland Independent Companies to be entirely different from other tartans so that the Black Watch policing force could not be associated with any particular clan.

A visit by King George IV in 1822 spurred a revival of Scottish national identity; alongside the romantic writings of Robert Burns and Walter Scott, a new interest in Highland culture and national dress emerged.

SCOTTISH TARTAN
Varies in colour and pattern depending on what natural dyes were available at the time it was established.

MODERN HIGHLAND GAMES

Take place all over the world.

This is when the invention of clan-specific tartan emerged.

When Queen Victoria came to the throne, she bought the now famous Balmoral Castle, and had it remodelled in a Scots baronial style. Prince Albert made great use of the Royal Stuart tartan for carpets, curtains and upholstery. The royal couple also designed their own tartan pattern and truly embraced Scottish life.

It seems ironic that as the nation was embracing Highland culture and taking on traditional Highland dress as a form of national identity, the first Highland clearances were taking place. Victoria and Albert continued to be visited by pipers and children dressed in Highland clothing, and the Prince hosted and enjoyed watching the Highland Games.

The original Highland Games allegedly date back to the 11th century, when King Malcolm III demanded a race to the summit of Craig Choinnich, in order to find the fastest runner to be his messenger. The events developed across the Highlands over the centuries and featured competitions such as tossing the caber, throwing the hammer and *maide leisg* (lazy stick).

Although many knew of, and competed in, such competitions, it wasn't until Victorian times that the Highland Games became properly organised, by Prince Albert. Ironically, this happened after most Highlanders had emigrated or had been removed from their land. What remained was the national identity (heavily reliant on tartan and kilts) and a revival of Scottish culture. Highland Games competitions are held throughout the world, the best known being the Cowal Highland Gathering, which happens every year in August near Dunoon, Scotland.

BALMORAL CASTLE
Became a royal residence in 1852 when it was purchased by Queen Victoria.

Edinburgh Castle

Edinburgh Castle is Scotland's most famous landmark. Positioned on top of the volcanic mound, Castle Rock, it dominates the Edinburgh skyline.

EDINBURGH CASTLE
Scotland's number one tourist attraction.

The first reference to Edinburgh castle is around AD 600, when it is referred to as Din Eidyn, a fortress on the rock. When the Angles captured Edinburgh in the Dark Ages, they renamed it Edinburgh. Although inhabitants have been recorded in this location since the 9th century, it wasn't until the 12th century, during the reign of David I, that the royal castle was built.

After King William 'The Lion' was forced to surrender the castle to the English in 1174, the castle changed hands and was fought over for hundreds of years, particularly during the Scottish Wars of

Independence and the Jacobite Risings. When Edward I attacked Scotland in 1296, the castle came under English control again. This time the English went a step further: Edward removed much of the castle's treasure, including the Scottish ceremonial coronation stone, the Stone of Scone. He had the stone built into a custom-made coronation chair to symbolise his power over Scotland.

Scotland regained control of the castle in 1329; after the English had fortified the castle following a second Scottish attempt at independence, the Scots finally managed to retake the castle after bluffing their way through the heavily guarded gates.

During the 15th century, the castle was built up and new features were added, including David's Tower, Crown Square and an expansion of the space available for arms manufacture.

After the failed Jacobite Rising of 1745, when Bonnie Prince Charlie reached the castle but failed to secure it for Scotland, the castle remained under British control; following the Treaty of Union in

HONOURS OF SCOTLAND
This famous crest features the crown, sword and sceptre.

STONE OF SCONE
Returned to Edinburgh in 1996.

MONS MEG

The giant cannon, or super gun, along with other armaments, was given as a gift to King James II by the Duke of Burgundy to celebrate James' wedding to his daughter. Mons Meg weighs 15,366 lb (6,970 kg) and is 15 ft (4.6 m) long. Each cannonball weighs 400 lb (181 kg) and it could be fired a maximum of 10 times per day, because of the heat created and the amount of gunpowder required. It was used briefly in battle and then on ceremonial occasions to mark the coronation of Scottish monarchs. It was put out of commission in 1680 when an operator loaded the charge incorrectly and the barrel burst – some believe this was done deliberately because the English did not have a cannon as big. After a brief spell in the Tower of London, Meg was returned to Edinburgh in 1829.

MONS MEG

1707, Scotland and England were now technically part of the same nation, Great Britain.

During the 18th century, Britain was involved in several wars, including the Seven Years' War, the American Wars of Independence and the

Napoleonic Wars. At this time the castle's vaults were used to hold prisoners and many new buildings and add-ons were erected. By 1811, it became clear that the castle vaults could not hold the prisoners, when 49 escaped through a hole in the south wall.

Since then, the castle has served as a national monument. When Walter Scott recovered the Scottish Crown Jewels in 1818, they were put on public display. The castle is now run by Historic Scotland as a tourist attraction and is the most popular place to visit in Scotland. It still has strong connections with the army and is used as a ceremonial post; the Edinburgh Tattoo is held on the ground every year and has become part of Scottish tradition.

CASTLE VAULTS
Were used to house prisoners captured during several European wars.

Global Citizens

When it comes to emigration, most people think of the Irish, but the Scots have also spread out all over the world, influencing many different cultures.

The Scots played in important role in the Indian subcontinent with many Highland regiments, including the famous Black Watch, assisting in putting down the Indian Mutiny of 1857. Nearly all Scottish churches sent missionaries to India and played a large part in the evangelisation and education of India. The interest in India stemmed from the rich trading opportunities, and the Scots, like the English, soon began to build colonies and bring their culture to India. Emigration was a two-way street and migrants from Asia soon began settling in Glasgow and Edinburgh, seeking a better life.

In China, William Jardine and James Matheson pioneered the successful opium trade that had begun in India. At this time,

the British East India Company monopolised trade and so Jardine saw an opportunity to expand the opium trade in China. He sent Matheson to investigate, and together they set up the hugely successful Jardine Matheson & Co. The firm's success was closely linked with the economic growth of Hong Kong and with trading in mainland China. China, like India, was a draw for Scottish settlers, who sent missionaries and scientists there.

Thomas Blake Glover is best known as the Scottish merchant who opened up trade between Japan and the rest of the world. He initially worked for Jardine Matheson, and then he set up his own business, the Glover Trading Co., selling weapons to the rebelling samurai clans. Unlike other western organisations, Glover sided with Japanese militants, eventually helping to bring down the Shogunate. Good relations created by Glover meant Scottish shipworkers in Aberdeen received the commission to build Japan's first warship. Glover was a key player in the industrialisation of

ALLEN OCTAVIAN HUME
A Scottish official in the Bengal Civil Service, a founder of the Indian National Congress, which led India to independence in 1947.

Japan, helping them develop coal mines and the shipbuilding company that later became Mitsubishi. For his contribution to Japan, he was awarded the Order of the Rising Sun – a national decoration established by the reigning Emperor Meiji.

Following the initial discovery of Nova Scotia in

Canada, thousands of emigrants, mainly Highlanders from the 'clearances', emigrated to Canada. Today, those of Scottish descent form the third-largest ethnic group in the country. Many of those who emigrated were unskilled

FLAG OF NOVA SCOTIA
This area of modern-day Canada was Scotland's first colony.

farmers who were attracted by a new life where they could keep their traditions and cultures without persecution.

By the end of the 18th century, Cape Breton Island had become a centre for Scottish settlement, where the only language spoken was Scots Gaelic. Several other areas became popular Scottish settlements – ironically, the British government was keen to send

Highland clans out of the country at a time when Scottish national identity and culture was being celebrated. Scottish culture is often said to be more alive and cherished in Canada than it is in Scotland, with clan gatherings and Highland games and the wearing of traditional tartan and kilts.

The Scots also have a presence in Australia and New Zealand, although many were transported there against their will as convicts. Some were sent on the pretext that it was punishment for a crime. However, most crimes were minor and this extreme punishment was more likely an excuse to send Highlanders away, as the government could no longer sustain their way of life.

MCGILL UNIVERSITY
In Montreal, Canada, was founded in 1821 by James McGill, who emigrated from Glasgow.

The Industrial Revolution

During the 19th century, Scotland's economy changed from one relying mainly on agriculture to one based on heavy industry.

Once trade began to open up with America, Africa and India, huge numbers of Scots were attracted to the riches of the growing urban centres and the opportunities they offered. The Scottish Enlightenment had also produced an outpouring of ideas and an interest in technology.

STEAM LOCOMOTIVES
The first successful locomotive line in Scotland ran between Monkland and Kirkintilloch.

As more raw materials and trade routes came through Scottish ports, merchants soon realised that goods could be manufactured for profit, and workers who had previously worked on the land

were now employed as weavers and factory labourers.

James Watt's invention of the steam engine transformed factories and was the driving force behind Scotland's industrial revolution. Machines were invented that changed the textile industry forever.

INDUSTRIALISATION
In New Lanark, cotton mills and houses sprang up on the banks of the River Clyde.

CHILD LABOUR

The industrial revolution meant that goods could be produced faster, cheaper and in large quantities. However, it also meant that workers were paid very little and families were often forced to send their children to work in factories and mines. Their small fingers meant they could reach inside tight spaces and operate fiddly machinery, but it also left them vulnerable to ill-treatment, poor pay and the danger of injury or death. It took until 1833 for the Factory Act to protect children's rights – it limited work to those aged 9 and over, made breaks and holidays compulsory and required time to be provided for education.

ABERDEEN ANGUS
Became famous worldwide thanks to improvements in transport.

Although the industrialisation of Scotland made factory owners and merchants extremely rich, the government was not prepared for the speed at which industry grew and the working class was poorly represented. Without the proper regulations, many people died in the unsafe working conditions of the factories and mines; they often faced beatings, long working days and extremely low pay.

Populations of the industrial towns sky-rocketed, which led to severe housing and health problems; combined with heavy pollution of the air and the water supply from the factories, life was dangerous for the average Scottish worker and his family. The invention of the steam engine created a huge demand for coal, and although coal had been used on a small scale for

GLASGOW
Quickly grew to become the second city of the British Empire.

SHIPBUILDING

Its geographical links to Motherwell and iron manufacturing meant that Glasgow quickly shifted its focus from the cotton industry to shipbuilding. Iron ships replaced their wooden predecessors and the invention of the steam engine made sails almost obsolete. Within just 40 years, the Clydebank area went from being uninhabited to housing over 30,000 people. Combined with its useful location, this made Glasgow a major seaport that was able to organise its many docks for more efficient trading.

centuries, a lot more was suddenly needed. Large-scale coal-mining sprang up all over the country with men, women, children and horses being sent to excavate the coal from the ground. The first mines were unregulated and problems with haulage, flooding and ventilation led to a catastrophic loss of life. It wasn't until 1842 that mine inspectors were appointed and women and girls were no longer allowed to work in mines; boys, however, were still able to work from the age of 10.

COAL-MINING
Was not regulated until 1842 and hundreds lost their lives.

The Scottish Engineers

JAMES WATT STATUE
At Greenock Town
Hall, Inverclyde.

Scotland has produced some of the most famous and important inventions in history, including the steam engine, the telephone and the MRI machine.

The increase in trade, particularly on the west coast of Scotland, created a need for navigational aids. Robert Stevenson, born in 1772, was an engineer and son of a merchant. He is famed for designing Scotland's first lighthouse, Little Cumbrae, and went on to supervise the construction of several more, including the Bell Rock Lighthouse near the entrance to the Firth of Tay – a particularly dangerous stretch of water that had claimed over 70 shipping vessels in one year alone. He was a key figure in the improvement of offshore warning systems and engineering difficulties created by increased traffic on roads, harbours and canals.

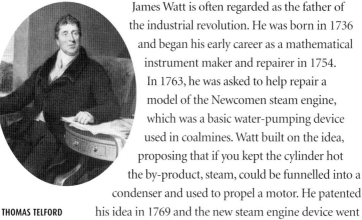

THOMAS TELFORD
Responsible for many of Britain's waterways.

James Watt is often regarded as the father of the industrial revolution. He was born in 1736 and began his early career as a mathematical instrument maker and repairer in 1754. In 1763, he was asked to help repair a model of the Newcomen steam engine, which was a basic water-pumping device used in coalmines. Watt built on the idea, proposing that if you kept the cylinder hot the by-product, steam, could be funnelled into a condenser and used to propel a motor. He patented his idea in 1769 and the new steam engine device went on to be used to drive machines in factories and in transport. By the 19th century, steam had become the main source of power in Britain.

James Clerk Maxwell was referred to by Einstein as 'the man who changed the world forever'; born in 1831, he studied at Cambridge University and later became a professor of physics. He is credited with discovering electromagnetism by showing how electric and magnetic forces travelled in waves. His discoveries

ROBERT STEVENSON
Designed Scotland's
first lighthouse.

laid the groundwork for future scientists and formulated the basis of hundreds of scientific theories. His discoveries led to the development of several modern technologies we still use today, including television, radio and radar.

As industry grew, there became a need for more organised road and water systems throughout the country. Thomas Telford, born in 1757, was a stonemason and civil engineer who became responsible for a number of canals, aqueducts and bridges throughout Britain. He designed over 30 bridges between 1792 and 1827, as well as many important roads; these helped to link Britain's towns and cities together as never before.

SAMUEL SMILES

Samuel Smiles is famous for his book, *Self-Help*, written in 1845. The book used the examples of successful Scottish engineers of the era as role models for self-improvement. This promoted a sort of national pride in the achievements of Scottish engineers and inventors at the time.

SCOTTISH ENGINEERING
The Scottish lighthouse invention was exported to Canada and helped reduce the disasters caused by the increase in maritime traffic.

Alexander Graham Bell was born in 1847 into a family fascinated with all things relating to speech. In the early 1870s, Bell emigrated to America, where he spent much of his free time trying to invent a machine that could send sound telegraphically – his initial aim was to enable deaf people to hear sounds this way. As a result, he came up with one of the world's most famous and useful inventions ever.

He patented his invention in 1876 and in 1877 founded the Bell Telephone Company. The popularity of the telephone was unprecedented and made Bell a multimillionaire. He went on to pioneer several other inventions, including optical telecommunications, hydrofoils and aeronautics.

Robert Louis Stevenson

Born in 1850, he was famous as the author of *Treasure Island, Kidnapped* and *The Strange Case of Dr Jekyll and Mr Hyde*.

ROBERT LOUIS STEVENSON
Scotland's most famous children's author.

Stevenson attended Edinburgh University and qualified as a lawyer, although he never practised. During his time at university he experimented with socialist and atheist ideas, much to his father's disapproval.

He was often ill as a child and suffered from tuberculosis. He spent most of his life travelling abroad to healthier climates and this inspired his first works, which were travel writings describing time spent canoeing and riding donkeys in France. He later travelled by sea to America and continued his travels across the South Pacific; the scenery of this foreign land gave him the inspiration for his first novel, *Treasure Island*.

Having previously been serialised in a children's magazine from 1881 to 1882, *Treasure Island* was published in book form in 1883. The novel described a search for buried treasure and pitted the forces of good (in the form of a boy, Jim, and his friends) against evil, personified by the one-legged pirate, Long John Silver.

The theme of good and evil continued in his next novel, *The Strange Case of Dr Jekyll and Mr Hyde*, this time within the same character. Dr Jekyll discovers a drug that transforms him into the evil monster, Mr Hyde, and the story follows his struggle to control the evil inside him.

TREASURE ISLAND
Was inspired by Stevenson's time spent in the South Pacific.

Stevenson went on to write a series of Highlander adventures, possibly inspired by the stories of the Covenanters told to him by his nanny. *Kidnapped* was published in 1886, followed by *The Black Arrow* and *The Master of Ballantrae* (1888). As well as adventure stories, Stevenson also wrote scientific essays, children's poetry and several autobiographical pieces.

Stevenson finally settled in Samoa, where

he died, most likely of a cerebral haemorrhage, in 1894. He had wanted his self-penned requiem to be inscribed on his tomb and, although slightly misquoted, he got his wish. His tomb read:

> *Under the wide and starry sky,*
> *Dig the grave and let me lie.*
> *Glad did I live, and gladly die,*
> *And I laid me down with a will.*
> *This be the verse you grave for me:*
> *'Here he lies where he longed to be;*
> *Home is the sailor, home from sea,*
> *And the hunter home from the hill.'*

DR JEKYLL
An illustration from the original edition of *The Strange Case Of Dr Jekyll and Mr Hyde.*

The poem was translated into Samoan and became a national song of grief that is still used to this day.

Stevenson was greatly admired by his contemporaries and has been an inspiration to the likes of Jorge Luis Borges, Ernest Hemingway, Rudyard Kipling, J. M. Barrie and G. K. Chesterton. However, after World War I his reputation dwindled when contemporary writers, including Virgina Woolf, criticised his work, caricaturing him as a writer of children's books and horror. Most of his other works were forgotten. Towards the end of the 20th century, his popularity was revived, with scholars looking at how his work reflected his social and humanist leanings. Stevenson remains popular today and is the 26th most translated author in the world.

ORIGINAL POSTER
Advertising one of thousands of stage adaptations of 'Jekyll and Hyde'.

The Forth Rail Bridge

1883 saw work begin on one of Scotland's finest engineering achievements, a bridge that linked Edinburgh with Dundee and Aberdeen by rail.

FORTH RAIL BRIDGE
Shown here
illuminated at night.

Following the Tay Bridge disaster of 1879, the original designer of the Forth Bridge, Thomas Bouch, was replaced by the engineers John Fowler and Benjamin Baker. Fowler and Baker designed a cantilever structure that was built by the Glasgow firm, Sir William Arrol and Co.

The bridge was built between 1883 and 1890 and was the longest single cantilever bridge in the world and the first major structure in Britain to be built out of steel.

The bridge measures 1.6 miles (2.5 km) in length and supports a double railway track that sits 151 ft

(46 m) above the water. The bridge is made up of four huge cantilever structures, each resting on a granite pier. In cantilever bridges, one portion of the bridge acts as an anchor that sustains another portion that extends beyond the supporting pier. The cantilever system was a major engineering breakthrough, as it could span great distances and be easily constructed off-site without having to construct temporary platforms for support; it also enabled engineers to calculate the forces and stresses that would be put on the girders. Although the cantilever design was not new, it had never been used on such a huge scale before.

BENJAMIN BAKER
Co-designer of
the Forth Rail Bridge.

Although the bridge was regarded as an engineering success, 63 men died during construction and many more were seriously injured when they fell into the water below. The bridge was finally opened in 1890 by Edward VII, who was prince at the time; he hammered in the last, gold-plated rivet. Since its first journey, thousands of trains have passed over the bridge without incident and up to 200 trains now cross the bridge each day.

THE TAY BRIDGE DISASTER

The designer of the Tay Bridge, Thomas Bouch, who prepared a proposal for the Forth Rail Bridge, was discredited in 1879 when the Tay Bridge collapsed during a violent storm while a train was passing over. The bridge was flawed in its design, and was not robust enough to withstand the strong winds of that night. There were no survivors and the total number of victims is unknown; only 46 bodies were recovered, but many more would have been on the train that night. The stumps of the original piers are still visible.

Tay Bridge collapses

Because of the unprecedented nature of the project, maintenance costs were not accounted for when it was first conceived. The heavy steam trains put constant stress on the bridge, to such an extent that a small

THE TAY BRIDGE
The original Tay Bridge before the collapse.

village of 50 houses and a workshop were constructed at nearby Dalmeny Station. The 'never-ending' repainting of the bridge has since become a local in-joke, perpetuating the myth that as soon as the bridge has been painted from one end to the other, it needs to be painted again. Painting of the bridge is lengthy, however, as was proved in 2011 when a painting job that started in 2002 was finally finished. At a cost of £130 million, the paint is expected to last at least 25 years before another coat is needed.

The Forth Rail Bridge appears on the 2004 issue of the pound coin and also on Scottish £20 banknotes. It has become an icon of industrial Scotland and has featured in films, books, advertising and video games; it was even awarded a Blue Peter badge in 2012.

NEW TAY BRIDGE
A second Tay Rail Bridge was completed in 1887.

The Antarctic

The Heroic Age of Antarctic Exploration during the early 1900s helped unearth important scientific discoveries from the region.

ROBERT FALCON SCOTT
Led the Discovery Expedition.

William Bruce launched the Scottish National Antarctic Expedition (SNAE) in 1902, which saw the completion of two voyages towards the South Pole. Sadly for Bruce, his focus on scientific discoveries was out of fashion at the time, and although he received less government backing than his rival, Robert Falcon Scott, his two missions were overwhelming successes. He succeeded in establishing a manned meteorological station and discovered new land; he also collected a large number of biological and geological samples, which led to the foundation of the Scottish Oceanographical Laboratory.

Bruce had already been on several Arctic and Antarctic expeditions as part of the Dundee Whaling Expedition and had initially applied to go on a different Antarctic expedition, which later became known as the Discovery Expedition. However, by the time his proposal had been assessed, he had progressed beyond the position he had applied for and instead proceeded independently with his own expedition.

Bruce planned to establish a meteorological station as near to the South Pole as possible in order to observe weather patterns; he also planned to conduct research into the geological and biological conditions of this uncharted area.

The first voyage left Scotland in 1902. After a near catastrophe at St Paul's Rocks in the Mid-Atlantic, the ship, the *SY Scotia*, made its final stop in the Falkland Islands before the last leg of its journey to the Antarctic.

It soon became stuck in pack ice and the crew faced treacherous conditions until they reached the South Orkney Islands. Here they constructed a stone building to provide shelter for those that would be left on the islands.

WILLIAM BRUCE
Scotland's unsung Antarctic hero.

RSS DISCOVERY
On show in Dundee.

The structure was named Ormond House, after Robert Ormond, Director of the Edinburgh Observatory, who had supported Bruce's project.

After some respite in Argentina, the crew set sail again in 1904. After reaching an ice barrier the crew tracked east and discovered new land. Bruce named it Coats' Land, after his main sponsors back in Scotland.

PIPER KERR

After discovering Coats' Land, Bruce's crew became stuck in pack ice again. The unforeseen standstill meant inactivity for the crew and it was during this time that one crew member, Gilbert Kerr, stepped out onto the ice with his bagpipes. He serenaded a local penguin and the photograph of this encounter was forever associated with the SNAE expedition.

Upon returning home, Bruce and his crew were showered with awards and medals. However, the rival expedition, the Discovery Expedition, led by Robert Falcon Scott, overshadowed Bruce's achievements, as did the later expedition by Shackleton. Bruce believed that this was a political move, since he had travelled independently and held some controversial Scottish nationalist beliefs, whereas Scott's mission was funded by the British government and, unlike Bruce, Scott claimed land and discoveries for Britain, rather than Scotland.

The Antarctic missions put the city of Dundee firmly on the map. The *RSS Discovery*, of the Discovery Expedition, was built by the Dundee Shipbuilding Company and was designed specifically for the freezing waters of the Antarctic. In fact, the original expeditions had been inspired by the 1893 Dundee Whaling Expeditions, during which time new land in Antarctica had been discovered and named Dundee Island. The *Discovery* is currently on display at Dundee Shipyard.

THE RSS DISCOVERY
Was specifically designed to navigate the icy waters of the Antarctic.

World War I

During the early 20th century, Scotland was in a deep recession. When the call came to fight in the Great War, many saw it as a way out.

The industrial revolution brought great change to Scotland, but from 1905 the economy became unstable as inflation grew out of control and the population boomed. By the time of the Great War in 1914, people were desperate to escape their lives of poverty. Men signed up to fight for Britain, lured by the promise of food and regular wages.

British propaganda had led the country to believe that the war would be easily won and, encouraged by this, thousands rushed to enlist.

Throughout World War I, the Royal Scots regiment sent 35 battalions to fight in France and lost 12,000 men. In total, Scotland lost over 100,000 men during the four years of fighting – these men are often referred to as the 'Lost Generation'.

GERMAN SOLDIERS
Surrender at Scapa Flow in 1918.

SCAPA FLOW

Scapa Flow is a large, natural harbour situated in Orkney. During the Great War it served as a safe port and was home to the British Grand Fleet. In 1916 the fleet came under attack when German forces invaded the trading waters between Scotland and Scandinavia. The British Navy met the German ships in the Battle of Jutland, when 6,000 men lost their lives.

As many historians have noted, the war was badly managed, with the generals in charge over-

A GREAT DEPRESSION
Followed The Great War – 30 per cent of Glaswegians were unemployed.

confident and ill-prepared for the struggle they would encounter. Those who did return from the front line had lost their faith in the politicians. Upon their return, not much had changed and most still faced poverty and unemployment; a plan to build a million new homes for 'returning heroes' fell woefully short. The global fallout of the war added salt to the wound. Britain's once booming industries began to collapse and the empire lost its position as a leading economic power. Britain faced a revolution and, for the first time in history, a Labour government presided over the nation's politics.

Because Scotland had relied on a fairly narrow industrial base, the Great Depression of 1920 hit the country hard. British industry could not compete with European competition and many lost their jobs or faced severely reduced hours. The Wall Street Crash of 1929 made matters even worse; by the 1930s, over one-third of the population was unemployed, with no welfare support to rely on.

For most, the only option for survival was either migration south for better job prospects, or – like the generation before – emigration to America, Canada or Australia. During this time, Scotland experienced mass emigration on a huge scale, much larger than that seen during the Highland clearances. Although some effort was made to generate interest and optimism in Scottish achievements through events like the 1938 Empire Exhibition in Glasgow, it wasn't until World War II that Scotland really came out of its economic slump.

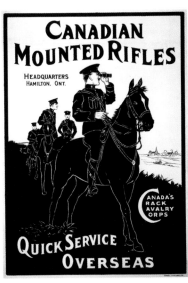

SCOTTISH EMIGRATION
Many Scots joined the Canadian Mounted Rifles.

WINSTON CHURCHILL
Became chancellor in 1924.

Red Clydeside

Between 1910 and the late-1930s, Glasgow, Paisley, Greenock and Clydebank became a centre for socialist ideals and political protests.

During the early 1900s, Scotland was suffering from an economic slump brought on by spiralling inflation. As a result, the booming population faced poverty and health problems and, on top of that, landlords were exploiting the situation to charge extortionate rents.

The first protests to take place in the Clydeside area were against the dramatic rent increases. In response, communities came together and organised a rent strike; 25,000 households refused to pay rent and the protesters formed defensive groups to protect those facing eviction. The strikes led to the first people-led political reform, the Rent Restriction Act of 1915. Together with pacifists, these political activists also saw how the threat of war could cause another great

WILLIE GALLACHER
The head of the
Clyde Workers'
Committee

blow to the Scottish economy, and in 1916 the Women's Peace Crusade organised the first march against the war.

By 1918 an organised group emerged, called Red Clydeside. Led by John MacLean and several others, the group campaigned for socialist principles such as freedom of speech, the right to protest and politics that should benefit 'all of mankind'.

The Bolshevik movement in Russia, in which peasants and working-class people were

DAVID LLOYD GEORGE
Led a Liberal government in Britain and passed a law banning engineers from leaving the company they worked for.

WOMEN'S RIGHTS

Notable women were involved in the Red Clydesiders; having been empowered by their contribution to the Women's Land Army and munitions factories during the war, women started getting involved in politics and protests. It was due to the work of Helen Crawford that the Rent Restriction Act was passed. Suffragists began campaigning for equal rights with men. By 1918, women over 30 were given the right to vote and were allowed, for the first time, to stand for parliament.

MARY BARBOUR
Became the first
female councillor
in Glasgow.

suffering at the hands of the elitist and corrupt Tsar Nicholas II, would have inspired the Red Clydeside movement. Encouraged by how groups of ordinary people had risen up and toppled a country's leader, the Red Clydeside movement organised their first rally on 31 January 1919; nearly 100,000 people gathered in George Square in the centre of Glasgow. They campaigned for regulated working hours and better working conditions. As in Russia, red flags were raised throughout the group; the red flag represented the communist idea that the needs of the majority should be represented in social policy.

The British government feared the protests, having seen how effective they were in Russia. The police read the Riot Act, which allows for specific orders to be given in threatening situations: 'When 12 or more people assemble unlawfully, they must disperse immediately or face disciplinary action'. The protesters did not disperse and the military was brought in to prevent the protest gaining momentum and turning into a revolution.

Although there was no revolution, Red Clydeside formed a major part of the labour movement in Britain, and in Scotland in particular. Red Clydeside replaced the Liberal Party as the representatives of the working class and, in 1922, several key figures were elected to the House of Commons. Since this time, the Labour Party has dominated Glasgow and its surrounding areas, although future Labour ministers would criticise the far-left ideals of the Red Clydesiders.

GEORGE SQUARE, GLASGOW
The scene of the biggest Red Clydeside rally, where 100,000 protesters gathered.

The Rise of Scottish Nationalism

The economic depression of the 1930s led to political unrest and widespread suffering, culminating in a resurgence of the Home Rule movement.

The 1930s was a period of mixed political feelings in Scotland, best expressed by Scottish writers and political activists such as Hugh MacDiarmid and John Buchan.

At this time, the Scots felt that the circumstances they now suffered in were a result of neglect by a government interested only in the concerns of London and southern England. Movements such as Red Clydeside led to left-wing politics being represented in government for the first time. Consequently, the Scottish departments for education, health and agriculture were moved from London to St Andrews. Although this gave Scotland more administrative independence than ever before, more and more Scots were calling for the separation of the United Kingdom and for Scotland

JOHN BUCHAN
Scottish Unionist whose writings inspired Unionist campaigners.

to be politically independent from England. In 1934, two groups joined together to form the Scottish Nationalist Party.

Scottish poet Hugh MacDiarmid was a modernist, communist and Scottish nationalist. In 1928 he helped form the National Party of Scotland; this was the forerunner of the Scottish National Party (SNP), which was formed in 1934. It was largely influenced by the Home Rule movement in Ireland, which saw the emergence of Sinn Féin. MacDiarmid, who was staunchly anti-English, was convinced that Scotland should be a republic state. Like many other nationalists, he believed that Scotland's interests would always suffer until it was able to control its own affairs both nationally and internationally.

JOHN MUIR
Observed the Scottish nationalist movement while developing his own controversial ideas in America.

The SNP did not, at first, campaign for a completely independent Scotland, but for a devolved Scottish parliament that would exist within the framework of the United Kingdom. The SNP, and MacDiarmid in particular, became influenced by the rise of facism in

Europe; however, unlike Hitler or Mussolini, Scottish nationalists were simply interested in controlling their own affairs and being separate from England.

Nationalism, however, was not the only political force influencing Scotland during the interwar years. On the other side of the fence were the Unionists, whose views were expressed in the novels of John Buchan, First Baron Tweedsmuir, who later served as governor general of Canada.

The Scottish Unionist Party was the main political party in Scotland from 1912 until 1965. They had close links with the Conservative Party but tried to keep this from the Scots people, instead claiming to be Liberals. Contrary to popular belief, the union referred to in the party's name was not the union between Scotland and England of 1707, but the Irish Act of Union 1801. The Scottish Unionists formed a pact with the controlling Conservative Party in England and focused on the connection between Scotland's union

SCOTTISH CABINET
Of the Fourth Scottish Parliament.

with the United Kingdom and the fate of its industry and economy. The majority believed that Scotland could not support itself economically unless it remained part of the United Kingdom.

Scotland was suffering from huge unemployment, poverty, health problems and widespread social unrest; some believed that being part of the United Kingdom and not having direct control over its affairs were to blame, whereas others believed that without the help of the United Kingdom, Scotland might end up in a worse situation altogether.

The arguments for and against devolution were put aside as another war broke out in 1939 and, once again, Scottish troops fought for Great Britain.

NATONALIST GRAFFITI
Scottish nationalist views spread throughout the country.

The State Will Provide

Scotland played an important part in the two wars and the years that followed saw the emergence of the welfare state and a better standard of living.

Scotland had been in an economic slump for decades until the Glasgow shipping and metalwork industries were called on once again to prepare for war. The Scots were responsible for the formation of the SAS and the invention of the Anderson Air Raid Shelter. The Women's Land Army in Scotland pioneered the Dig For Victory campaign, which encouraged women and children to help harvest local produce. Women also worked in factories and various volunteer services.

Before the war, Scotland's housing was severely inadequate and social provision could not keep up with the boom of the industrial revolution; many lived in overcrowded slums. War damage had made living conditions even worse; finally, something had to be done. During the late 1940s and early 1950s, metropolitan boroughs were added to major

WILLIAM BEVERIDGE
The father of the welfare state, who believed the government should look after those in need.

cities, including Glasgow, Dundee and Edinburgh. The housing crisis was stemmed, but not solved, and schemes to build entirely new towns were launched. The first was East Kilbride, which is now one of Scotland's biggest towns; this was followed by Glenrothes, Cumbernauld, Livingston and Irvine.

These new towns attracted new businesses, including development agencies, the Inland Revenue and several electronic companies.

The biggest change for Scotland, and for the rest of the United Kingdom, was the introduction of the welfare state. It had become apparent that people were living in poverty and were in need of support from the state. William Beveridge compiled a report outlining the five main social problems that he believed the state had ultimate responsibility for: want, disease, ignorance, squalor

RAVENSCRAIG STEELWORKS
A direct result of welfare reforms.

TALBOT AVENGER
One of the last cars
produced at the
Linwood factory.

and idleness. He argued that through social policy, the government should ensure that all people had access to adequate income, health care, education, housing and employment. He proposed that all those who worked should pay a 'national insurance' that would help provide support for those who were sick, unemployed or retired. Beveridge's reforms were introduced by the Labour Party, following their victory in 1945, and for the first time Britain had a benefit system that included free health care and child support payments.

Although the welfare state remains controversial, the system has brought about a dramatic reduction in the incidence of poverty and is a model that has been copied throughout much of the developed world.

After World War II and the introduction of the new welfare state model, the United Kingdom's economy and industry boomed once again. The state fulfilled its role in providing employment and housing and expanded manufacturing plants, such as Ravenscraig Steel Works and Linwood car factory; this era was characterised by projects such as the building of the Forth Road Bridge. Capitalism dominated and new employment opportunities enabled more and more people to join the middle classes.

However, Scotland's traditional industries, such as shipbuilding and coal-mining, were failing faster than the new industries could be set up. This led once again to widespread unemployment and the Labour government's failure to control the situation brought about a resurgence of SNP ideas that had been abandoned since before World War II.

FORTH ROAD BRIDGE
Represents economic growth during Scotland's golden age of capitalism.

Whisky Galore

It has been the national drink of Scotland for centuries, but it wasn't until the 18th century that commercial distilleries began producing whisky.

Some historians think that the practice of distilling whisky dates back to the time of the ancient Celts. The Celts were known to produce a fiery liquid called *uisge beatha*, meaning 'water of life', and it is this first offering that evolved into Scotch whisky.

WHISKY'S ORIGIN
Could date back to 11th-century monks.

By the 11th century, monks made their own whisky in distilleries built in the grounds of their monasteries, with each drink bearing the name of the monastery and tasting uniquely different.

As the popularity of the drink rose, government saw an opportunity and, in 1644, the first tax was levied; this resulted in hundreds of illegal distilleries springing up around the country.

George IV's visit to Scotland in 1822 prompted a revival of Scottish culture and national identity. The Excise Act a year later eased restrictions on the production of whisky and made illegal distilleries more difficult to operate – the popularity of whisky increased, the processes were refined and the drink became smoother.

MALT WHISKY

Malt whisky

Most Scotch whisky is either single or blended malt whisky, which means that the drink can only be made from malted barley. Malting is a process in which grains (in this case, barley) are soaked in water until they germinate. The germination process releases enzymes within the grain that break down starches and convert them into sugar. Many distilleries in Scotland have their own malting facilities, including Glenfiddich, Laphroaig, Highland Park, Glen Ord and Balvenie.

Whisky is made by drying either the malted barley, in the case of malt whisky, or other grains, in the case of grain whisky; the grains are either dried with hot air, or, in some cases, smoked. The dried grain is ground into a flour product called grist, which is then mixed in a huge drum called a 'mash tun'. Yeast is added and the mixture is left to ferment. Finally, the liquid is distilled – this process filters out impurities and increases the alcohol content. Most distilleries will distil their whisky at least twice for purity of flavour.

GELNMORANGIE
This distillery produces some of Scotland's most famous single malt whisky.

The whisky is then left in oak barrels to mature; it must mature for at least three years if it is to be called Scotch whisky. Like wine, whiskies will need different lengths of time to mature, depending on the year of distillation. As a rule, older whiskies are considered superior, and their scarcity means that they often sell at a very high price.

Scotch whisky is now regulated by the Scotch Whisky Regulations. Here are some terms to help understand the origins and nature of the different types:

Regions – the four main regions and their most famous distilleries are: The Highlands, Lowlands, Campbeltown and Islay.

Single malt Scotch – As mentioned previously, malt whisky can only be produced from barley, so in this case the word 'single' refers to the distillation process – meaning it was made from malted barley and distilled in one pot.

Blended malt Scotch – this is a blend of two or more single malt Scotch whiskies from different pots or distilleries; even though it is blended, because it is malt, it will all derive from barley.

Single grain Scotch – again, the word 'single' refers to the distillation process, meaning it has been distilled in one pot. The use of the word 'grain' means that it has been made from a mixture of grains.

Blended grain Scotch – this is a mixture of two or more single grain Scotch whiskies that have been blended from different pots of distilleries.

Blended Scotch – a mixture of single malt and single grain whiskies.

WHISKY BARRELS
At the Kilchoman Distillery, Islay.

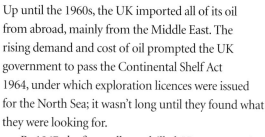

North Sea Oil

The discovery of oil off the north-east coast of Scotland transformed that area of the country and created a profitable new industry for Scotland.

NORTH SEA OIL
An offshore oil platform in north-east Scotland.

Up until the 1960s, the UK imported all of its oil from abroad, mainly from the Middle East. The rising demand and cost of oil prompted the UK government to pass the Continental Shelf Act 1964, under which exploration licences were issued for the North Sea; it wasn't long until they found what they were looking for.

By 1967, the first well was drilled. Huge companies, including BP and Shell, soon got on board and North Sea oil platforms sprang up to the north and east of the Scottish mainland. Later, further oil fields were discovered to the east of the Orkney and Shetland Islands. Aberdeen soon became the centre of Britain's oil industry, with many oil terminals being built along the coast to support the workers and infrastructure of the oil industry.

By 1973, the oil crisis created by the Arab-Israeli war led to another period of high inflation, unemployment and recession in Scotland.

During the 1970s and beyond, it became clear to Scotland that it was the only country to have struck oil, and yet become poorer. Their neighbour, Norway, had also exploited the oil fields in its areas of the North Sea, and this had resulted in a dramatic impact on their standard of living and a boom in technology, industry and advances in new forms of 'green' energy.

OIL TERMINALS
Were built to support the industry on the north-east coast of the Scottish mainland and on the Orkney and Shetland Islands.

YOM KIPPUR WAR
Also known as the
Arab-Israeli war,
caused economic
problems and affected
the price of oil.

The Scottish National Party (SNP) believed that it now made even more sense than ever to be independent from England. They believed that the discovery of oil and the revenue it brought in would not benefit Scotland as long as the United Kingdom and a government in Whitehall controlled the industry.

The 1974 general election won a majority for the Labour Party, led by Harold Wilson. At the same time, Scottish support for the SNP had been growing. The SNP gained seven seats in the House of Commons, commanding 30 per cent of Scottish votes. Their slogan, 'It's Scotland's Oil', summed up the general feeling at that time.

Government plans, only revealed in 2005, showed that ministers feared growing Scottish nationalism and the loss of a huge tax surplus in Scotland that would be created from oil revenue. The UK government needed the revenue from Scotland's oil to recover from recession and to pay for involvement in wars overseas.

In 1979, a referendum was held asking Scots if they wanted to establish a devolved legislature for Scotland.

When 52 per cent voted yes, Whitehall insisted that the 52 per cent only counted as 32 per cent, because of a loophole that counted foreign students, the recently deceased and abstainers as 'no' voters.

Although Scotland does still receive higher public spending per capita than the rest of the UK, nationalists still believe that the billions earned from oil obtained in Scottish waters have been used to fund matters more important to the English, and in recent years to bail out the economy following the credit crunch of 2008. It didn't help that Tony Blair's Labour government moved the boundary of the North Sea, making 6,000 square miles of Scottish sea English.

Figures show that if Scotland were to gain independence, it would have a budget surplus of nearly £6 billion.

THE NORTH SEA
Ownership of the sea around Scotland has been disputed by England and Scotland for centuries.

Banks and Finance

The Royal Bank of Scotland is synonymous with Scottish finance and, since its foundation in the 18th century, has gained a global presence.

RBS HEADQUARTERS, EDINBURGH
The home of RBS was built in 1774 by Sir Lawrence Dundas.

The 1707 Act of Union led to political unrest in Scotland, which culminated in the Jacobite Risings. The 'old' or 'original' Bank of Scotland sympathised and helped to fund the early Jacobite rebellions. The Royal Bank of Scotland was established by the English parliament in order to provide a financial centre in Scotland with strong ties to Hanoverian rule.

At this time, Scotland was in financial difficulty because of the failed Darien Scheme expeditions. As part of the new United Kingdom of Great Britain it relied heavily on financial support from England.

When the Royal Bank of Scotland first opened its doors, it faced heavy competition from the Bank of Scotland; the two banks competed with each other by collecting each other's banknotes and then exchanging them in return for payment. The banks finally agreed that these tactics would eventually lead to self-destruction and in the end each agreed to accept the other's banknotes.

Throughout the late 18th century, the Royal Bank of Scotland expanded its empire, opening branches in Glasgow, Dundee, Greenock and Leith. It went from strength to strength, merging with smaller Scottish banks, and acquiring further assets from the Western Bank and the Dundee Banking Company.

As the British Empire continued to grow, the Royal Bank of Scotland seized the opportunity to open a branch in London, which had become the financial centre of the Empire. The bank's presence grew again in the early 20th century as

SCOTTISH NOTES
Feature a different design from English notes.

MARGARET THATCHER
Funded her reforms with Scottish money.

FINANCIAL CRISIS
Of 2008 saw shares
in RBS tumble to
an all-time low.

it took on some small English banks. Then, in 1969, it merged with the National Commercial Bank of Scotland, making it the largest clearing bank in Scotland.

It was at this time that the bank took on the iconic logo of four inward-pointing arrows; the arrows represent the accumulation and concentration of wealth by the newly named RBS Group PLC.

Although the Bank of England took over banknote production in Northern Ireland and Wales, Scottish banks retained their right to issue their own notes. There are three different types of Scottish notes in circulation today, those printed by the Royal Bank of Scotland, as well as Bank of Scotland and Clydesdale Bank notes.

The RBS Group built on their earlier success during the latter half of the 20th century and into the 21st century, acquiring NatWest, Ulster Bank and providing the service behind WorldPay, as well as sponsoring sports people and sporting events, such as the Williams Formula 1 team, the RBS Six Nations Cup and the Scottish tennis player, Andy Murray.

The bubble burst in 2008 when RBS, like many other banks, oversold mortgages and lending options and were hit hard by the global financial crisis. Following an unprecedented bailout, 84 per cent of RBS is now owned by the UK taxpayer (government), who bought £45 billion worth of stock. It subsequently fell dramatically in value and by 2011 a loss of £26 billion had been made. RBS went on to cause more controversy in 2011 when they paid out nearly £1 billion in banker's bonuses while reporting losses of £1.1 billion.

RBS LOGO
Featuring four inward-pointing arrows represents the accumulation and concentration of wealth.

Other Scottish financial institutions did not suffer the same misfortune and remain well-respected in the financial industry: Scottish Widows, which has been around since 1815, is the most trusted pensions and investment provider, and Standard Life PLC is a global savings and investment business with over 6 million customers worldwide.

High Tech Edge

Scotland's heavy industries had been in decline since the 1980s, but with the growth in electronics and IT, a new technological age dawned.

The Scottish Development Agency was set up in the 1970s to help stimulate economic growth by developing new ideas for business and investment. New technology businesses set up shop across Scotland's Central Belt, which earned it the nickname Silicon Glen. There was a huge emphasis on design and technological innovation.

Two of Scotland's most famous exports in this field today are Dolly the Sheep and Rockstar Games. Dolly the Sheep was the first mammal to be successfully cloned and was an achievement made possible by

DUNDEE
An important major city and home to Rockstar Games.

the scientists of the Roslin Institute, near Edinburgh. Dolly was born in 1996 and was an exact duplicate of the adult donor of the original cell. The embryologist in charge, Dr Ian Wilmut, received a knighthood for his scientific breakthrough. Dolly lived for only six years and died of a progressive lung disease; it is not known whether this was a result of the cloning. Her taxidermy body can be seen on display at the National Museum of Science in Edinburgh.

DOLLY THE SHEEP
At the Museum of Science, Edinburgh.

Rockstar Games grew out of DMA Design Ltd, a video game development company founded in Dundee by David Jones. DMA's first major success was with the popular platform game, *Lemmings*; they then went on to produce games for all popular games consoles. After mergers and wranglings with various companies, including Nintendo and Sony BMG, Rockstar Games emerged in 1997 with their

FALKIRK WHEEL

A visual representation of Scotland's engineering heritage and recent technological advances.

groundbreaking video game, *Grand Theft Auto*. Rockstar North, as it is now known, is based in Edinburgh and is responsible for many well-known games, including: the *Grand Theft Auto* series, the *Max Payne* series, *L.A. Noire*, *Red Dead Redemption*, *The Ballad of Gay Tony*, the *Manhunt* series and *Agent*.

THE FALKIRK WHEEL

In 2002, Scotland's technological advances combined with its engineering past when scientists and engineers developed the Falkirk Wheel. This rotating boat-lift connects the Forth and Clyde Canal to the Union Canal. Before its introduction, boats had to process through a set of 11 locks, whereas now they are simply lifted up from the Forth and Clyde to the Union Canal. Officially opened by Queen Elizabeth II in 2002, it has become a symbol of 21st-century Scottish engineering.

Scotland has also become a key player in the green energy revolution. Green technology has become of central importance to modern Scotland. Wind turbines can be seen across the hills of Scotland and they often provide enough energy to power entire communities. In some cases, such as the Isle of Gigha, energy not used by the community is sold back to the national grid.

ROCKSTAR GAMES
This pioneering video games company is based in Scotland.

Scotland is at the forefront of green technology and leads the way in tidal and hydroelectric technology. While hydroelectric dams, such as Pitlochry and Cruachan, have been generating electricity for years, Scotland has now installed floating generators in the North Sea that convert wave movement into electricity.

Rain is plentiful in Scotland and almost all of the larger rivers can be used to generate power. Perhaps Scotland's future revenue lies in selling back the 'green' energy it has generated.

Culture

Scotland has retained a lot of its cultural traditions – many dating back as far as the Celtic times.

J. M. BARRIE
Famous author of *Peter Pan*.

Even after the Treaty of Union in 1707, Scotland still maintained its unique Scots law and the Church of Scotland, which never merged with the Church of England.

Scotland is well known for its food and is often the butt of jokes about high-calorie food, especially since a chip shop in Scotland invented the concept of a deep-fried Mars bar. However, other Scottish dishes include haggis, which is a traditional dish of offal mixed with oatmeal and spices encased in a sheep's stomach – it is traditionally eaten with 'neeps and tatties'; haggis most likely dates back to the time of Highland cattle drivers who needed high-calorie rations to take with them on their long journey to Edinburgh. Other Scottish dishes include salmon, venison, cranachan, Scotch broth and shortbread.

In sport, Scotland competes both as part of Great Britain and as a separate nation. Their rugby team is one of the best in the world, as are its golfers and famous golf courses. Scotland has its own national sport, shinty, which is similar to the Irish sport of hurling, as well as curling, which is like bowls played on ice.

Since the 20th century, the world of media has expanded rapidly and, despite being part of the United Kingdom, Scotland has several of its own newspapers, radio shows and TV channels.

During the 1990s, Scottish pop music became part of the mainstream UK media, with people embracing the sounds of Shamen and Primal Scream. Wet Wet Wet had one the most successful pop songs ever, *Love is All Around*, and as Indie music became more popular, Travis and Belle & Sebastian made names for themselves internationally.

In the world of film, several Scottish actors, comedians and writers have become famous worldwide. Mel Gibson's 1995 film, *Braveheart*,

FRANZ FERDINAND
One of Scotland's most famous rock bands.

BAGPIPES

Bagpipes have become synonymous with Scotland but, contrary to popular belief, they are not believed to have been used widely in Scotland up until the 18th century – although there is some evidence that they date back to the 14th century. The surge in popularity came when pipers were recruited into the military. Since then they have been used ceremonially at funerals, marches and memorials, especially within military and police establishments.

BAGPIPES
The national
instrument
of Scotland.

was a huge box-office hit and brought Scottish history to a global audience. Other films set in Scotland, such as *Shallow Grave* and *Trainspotting*, painted an entirely different picture of modern-day Scotland, particularly Edinburgh. Many famous actors have come from Scotland, including Ewan McGregor, Sean Connery, Robert Carlyle, John Barrowman, Robbie Coltrane, Billy Connolly, Brian Cox, Alan Cumming, Henry Ian Cusick, Deborah Kerr, Simone Labibe, James McAvoy, Dougray Scott, David Tennant and Richard Wilson.

Scotland's major cities, and the beautiful scenery of the lochs, glens and islands, are popular tourist attractions. Ben Nevis is the highest mountain in the British Isles – situated to the western end of the Grampians, it attracts over 100,000 climbers per year.

Scotland has a long and distinguished line of artistic and literary greats, from the first Makars through to Robert Burns and Robert Louis Stevenson. More recently, Scotland's latest successful writer has emerged: J. K. Rowling, author of the Harry Potter novels, who hails from Edinburgh. In the art world, the Museum of Scotland opened in Edinburgh in 1998, bringing together many interesting Scottish artefacts, as well as displaying contemporary artworks from around the world.

KELVINGROVE ART GALLERY
In Glasgow is Scotland's most visited free attraction.

NATIONAL GALLERY, SCOTLAND
Has almost 4,000 different artworks over three sites.

Independence or Union?

Since 1968, Scotland's status within the United Kingdom has become a hotly debated topic and a major issue that drives Scottish politics.

HOUSES OF PARLIAMENT
Much of Scotland is still controlled by Westminster.

Since the discovery of oil off the coast of Scottish land in the 1960s, many Scottish nationalists have become even more convinced that Scotland would be better off controlling its own politics.

During the 1980s, Magaret Thatcher's Conservative government used North Sea oil as a major funding source to balance an economy crippled by the Arab-Israeli war and also to pay for the costs of reform. By 1984, the government proposed the closure of 174 state-owned mines, many of which were in Scotland.

The majority of miners went on strike and faced strong opposition from Thatcher's unrelenting policies. The eventual closure of 150 mines across the UK resulted in the loss of thousands of jobs. In towns where mining had been the main source of income entire communities collapsed. Miners were forced to call off the strike in 1986 and mining towns, such as those in Fife, Stirlingshire and Lanarkshire, lost most of their pits and their main source of employment. Today, only a few privately owned mines remain.

HOLYROOD
Scottish parliament buildings (known as Holyrood), Edinburgh.

Thatcher fuirther alienated the growing nationalist movement in Scotland when her government introduced the community charge (or poll tax) in Scotland in 1989, and in England and Wales a year later. The poll tax was one of Thatcher's most unpopular policies and its introduction led to full-scale riots in London.

Thatcher will always be a controversial topic in Scotland; for some she is the saviour who dug Britain out of yet another recession and re-established the UK as a world power. However, many believe that Scotland's industries were relied on too heavily to foot the bill and many of the social problems experienced by the working classes were a result of Thatcher's economic policies, which sought to make the rich richer and, at the same time, offered less help to those in need of state benefits.

EDINBURGH FESTIVAL
Attracts visitors from around the world.

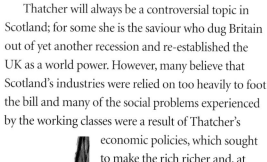

A devolution bill had been voted on in 1979 and, despite a majority voting yes, the controversial loophole meant Scotland was still controlled by a Whitehall government. Thatcher's 'New Right' government had alienated her Conservative supporters in Scotland and in 1997, New Labour's overwhelming victory and greater representation in Scotland saw a second devolution referendum. This time the vote was a decisive yes.

The first reconvened Scottish Parliament met in 1999 at Holyrood in Edinburgh. This meant that the SNP could now firmly establish its political force in Scotland and gained 35 seats in the Scottish parliament.

In 2007 the SNP became the largest party represented in government, and by 2011 it had won 69 seats. The question of whether Scotland should be an independent nation was decided at a referendum in 2014, when the Scottish electorate decided either for or against continuing union with the United Kingdom. Scotland said no to independence by 55.3% to 44.7%.

The SNP won a landslide victory in the 2015 General Election, with 56 out of 59 MPs elected to Westminster and also won 63 seats in the 2016 Scottish Parliamentary elections, losing its overall majority.

At the EU Referendum in June 2016, Scotland voted overwhelmingly to remain in the EU by 62% to 38%, increasing calls for a further independence vote.

The snap General Election of 2017 resulted in the SNP remaining the largest party, retaining 35 of the 56 seats won two years earlier. However, 21 seats were lost. The Conservatives doubled their share of the vote and won 13 seats while Labour and the Liberal Democrats took 7 and 4 seats respectively.

Index

Acknowledgments

Picture credits

Photos.com: p. 6 Ai-Lan Lee, 7 Rudolf Kotulajn , 9 Jonathan Maddock, 12 Mike Clark, 13 Jupiterimages, 15 Lars Johansson, 22 Juliane Jacobs, 24 Victor Lord Denovan, 27 William McKelvie, 30 Greg McKinnon, 32 Clifford Shirley, 35 Hazel Proudlove, 37 Igor Kisselev, 40 Collpicto, 43 Angus Forbes, 46 Photos.com, 50(t) William McKelvie, 50(b) Thorsten Schmitz, 51(b) Michael Palis, 53(t) Photos.com, 55 Photos.com, 56 Alan Crawford, 60 Denise Jones, 64(t) Bertrand Collet, 64(b) Jupiterimages, 65 Phil Dickson, 68 Victor Lord Denovan, 75(b) Jaime Pharr, 76 Lesley Jacques, 78 Chris Green, 79 Melanie Braun, 86 Georgios Kollidas, 91(b) Photos.com, 95 Jakich, 97(t) Georgios Kollidas, 99 Aaron MacDougall, 100 William McKelvie, 101 William McKelvie, 102 Daniel Mytens, 105 Achim Prill, 107 Ai-Lan Lee, 108 Photos.com, 109(t) John Braid, 109(b) Chris Hepburn, 113 Photos.com, 122 Mike Bentley, 131 pdiaz, 137(t) Michael Milton, 138 Carl Millar, 142 Photos.com, 146 Carl Millar, 149 Jupiterimages, 152 David Woods, 154 Photos.com, 155 Steve Baxter, 156 James Martin Greenshields, 157 Paul Cowan, 159(b) Inga Sõelsepp, 160 Angus Forbes, 161 Stuart Murchison, 163 Photos.com, 165 David Woods, 166 Hugh McKean, 168 Eli Franssens, 170 Photos.com, 171 Iain McGillivray, 173(l) setimino, 177 Andrew Barker, 178 William McKelvie, 182 Jeremy Richards, 185 Photos.com, 187 Photos.com, 188(t) Tracy Fox, 188(b) Jupiterimages, 189 Photos.com, 193 Ivelin Ivanov, 198 Stockbyte, 199 Photos.com, 201 Iain Jaques, 204 Paula Jones, 221 Stephen Wilson, 223 tarczas, 226 Flavijus Piliponis, 227 Tomas Sereda,

229 Joe Gough, 230 John Pavel, 231(t) Comstock Images, 234 Rae_The_Sparrow, 241(t) David Woods, 241(b) Kevin Eaves, 242 fazon1.

Wikipedia: p. 17, 18, 19, 23, 25, 29(t), 29(b), 31, 39, 41(t), 41(b), 42, 47, 48, 49, 51(t), 52, 53(b), 54, 58, 62, 63(b), 69, 70, 71, 72, 73, 74, 75(t), 80(t), 82, 83, 84, 85, 87(t), 87(b), 89, 90, 91(t), 92, 93, 94, 97(b), 103, 106, 112, 115, 116, 117, 118, 120, 123, 126, 127, 128, 129, 130, 134, 135, 136, 137(b), 139, 140, 143, 145, 147, 148, 150, 151, 153, 158, 159(t), 162, 167, 169(t), 172, 173(r), 174, 175, 176, 179, 180, 183, 184, 190, 191, 192, 194, 195, 196, 197, 200, 202, 203, 207, 208, 209, 210, 211, 212, 214, 215, 216, 217, 218, 219, 220, 224, 225, 228, 231(b), 232, 233, 235, 236, 237, 238, 239, 240, 243, 244, 245

Jim Linwood/Flickr: p.59

Clipart.com: p. 7, 28

RCAHMS / SCRAN: p. 63

TPL: p. 8, 10, 14, 16, 20-21, 26, 32-33, 34, 36, 38(t), 38(b), 44-45, 57, 61, 63(t), 66-67, 77, 80-81, 88, 96, 98, 104, 110-111, 114, 119(t), 119(b), 121, 124, 125, 132, 133, 141, 144, 164, 169(b), 181, 186, 205, 206, 213, 222

Illustrations by: Anthony Morris, Lucy Su, Robin Lawrie, John Rabou and James Field

Cover

photos.com: George Doyle, Christopher Sharratt, Stefan Nielsen, John Pavel, Steven Wynn, George Kollidas, Krzch-34, Flavijus Piliponis, Sue Colvil, Stepehn Finn, Briget McGill, Wheeman76, Wendy Conway, Juliane Jacobs, Judith Mainwaring, James Wilson, Vichie81, Valeria Potapova, Serhiy Shullye, Stuart Infante de Anglais

Every effort has been made to trace copyright holders not mentioned here. If there have been any omissions, we will be happy to rectify this in a reprint.

Gill Books
Hume Avenue, Park West, Dublin 12

www.gillbooks.ie

Gill Books is an imprint of M.H. Gill & Co.

Copyright © Teapot Press Ltd 2013

ISBN: 978-0-7171-5372-5

This book was created and produced by Teapot Press Ltd

Editor: Mel Plehov
Consultant editor: Dr Mark Jardine
Design: Tony Potter and Alyssa Peacock
Copy-editor: Fiona Biggs

Printed in EU

This book is typeset in Minion & Dax